Criminal Justice:
The Way Ahead

Part 3: Modernising the Criminal Justice System

Annexes

Introduction

1   There never has been a golden age when everyone in our society has been able to live their life free from crime, and free from the fear of crime.

2   But, over much of the last quarter of a century, crime has had an increasingly pervasive – and corrosive – effect on our society. It restricts basic civil liberties and undermines the social bonds integral to strong communities. The factors which led to the rise in crime are complex. But there can be little doubt that contributory factors include the collapse of employment opportunities especially for unskilled men, an explosion in hard drug abuse, a great rise in the availability of higher value, consumer goods, and widespread changes in social attitudes.

3   Confronting these issues and creating a more responsible society is a task beyond the criminal justice system alone. It requires concerted action across Government, in local communities, in schools and homes. But an effective, well-run criminal justice system (CJS) can obviously make a significant difference to levels of offending and crime.

4   Such a criminal justice system must be:

- effective at preventing offending and re-offending;

- efficient in the way it deals with cases;

- responsive at every stage to the needs of the victims and the law abiding community; and

- accountable for the decisions it takes.

In other words, a criminal justice system which delivers justice for all.

5   A great deal of work has already been made to secure effective cooperation between the police and local communities; to target those crimes of particular public concern; and to bring the often disparate criminal justice agencies together to work as part of a single, more coherent system. But radical reform of the CJS is a long-term project. So, the Government has given early priority to reforming those parts of the system in most urgent need of change.

6   Profound improvement is already underway. Following an inquiry under Sir Iain Glidewell, the Crown Prosecution Service (CPS) has been restructured, its areas made coterminous with police force areas, with more local Chief Crown Prosecutors, and with a greater focus it on its core business of prosecuting cases. After years of under-investment, a 23 per cent real term rise in funding for 2001-02 is enabling the CPS to begin the recruitment of scores of extra prosecutors.

7   The youth justice system is also being transformed. The establishment of a national Youth Justice Board, and a network of local Youth Offending Teams, is coordinating effort against youth crime as never before. Repeat cautioning of juveniles has ended, and new Final Warnings are providing effective early intervention to divert youngsters from crime. Graduated court sanctions are helping to ensure that young offenders, and their parents, take greater responsibility for their behaviour, and allow for the active involvement of the victims in the process.

8   Statutory Crime and Disorder Reduction Partnerships between the police, local councils, the health service and voluntary organisations have been established across the country to ensure that everyone plays their part in reducing crime. They are benefiting from a three-year Crime Reduction Programme – including the biggest ever expansion of CCTV this country has seen – to help drive crime down at a local level. New anti-social behaviour orders are bringing peace and quiet to many neighbourhoods, while more than 1,100 successful prosecutions have taken place for new offences of racial violence and racial harassment.

Introduction

9 The Probation Service has been reorganised into a single national service beginning in April 2001, again with 42 areas, coterminous with the police. From the same date, magistrates' courts will also be reorganised into the same 42 coterminous areas. The Prison Service is investing large sums into drugs prevention, accredited offending behaviour programmes and better education and training.

10 A range of programmes across Government is helping to tackle the underlying causes of crime, from Sure-Start for pre-school children, the new 'Connexions' programme and the Children's Fund, Welfare to Work, through to substantial programmes within and outside the CJS to tackle drug abuse.

11 These changes – and many more – are bearing fruit. The British Crime Survey (BCS) is the largest and most authoritative survey of overall levels of crime. It showed a ten per cent drop in crime between 1997 and the end of 1999. This included big falls in the targeted crimes of burglary and car crime (21 per cent and 15 per cent respectively).

12 This recent success is a testament to the dedication of those who work in the CJS, and to the many thousands of volunteers and community groups who play such a crucial role in making our society safer.

13 Yet crime is still far higher than it was 20 years ago. And, although the BCS suggests that violent crime overall has fallen, robbery and street crime have risen. Moreover, the demands on the police – not least from increasing public expectations and easier communications (such as mobile phones) – are rising.

14 Alongside all this, the nature of crime is constantly evolving. We know that a substantial proportion of property crime is fuelled by drugs misuse, while evidence suggests that a hardcore of about 100,000 offenders are responsible for about a half of all crime. Crime is also increasingly becoming more organised and international in character, and the continuing advances in communications technology will provide further opportunities for criminal behaviour.

15 Over the last 20 years the chances of an offender being brought to book for his or her crimes have fallen dramatically. Less than a quarter of crimes recorded by the police now end in an offender being brought to justice. Four fifths of persistent offenders are reconvicted within two years of finishing a prison sentence or starting probation supervision.

16 The formal system of justice needs to reflect the common sense all of us share about the best way to deal with wrong-doing in our everyday lives: like the importance of laying down clear and unambiguous rules; responding immediately and consistently if those rules are broken; and making sure that the punishment fits the criminal as well as the crime and gets more demanding if misbehaviour persists.

17 Nothing does more damage to people's confidence in the CJS than a perception that criminals are getting away with their crimes. Why report a crime if there is little prospect of seeing a criminal convicted? Why come forward as a witness if the system cannot protect your interests as well as those of the defendant?

18 We are therefore committed to raise further the performance of the CJS and, in doing so, raise the confidence of the public, and of those who work in the CJS. Fundamental to achieving this are two key components: fundamental reform and large-scale investment.

19   Last year we announced the biggest investment in the CJS for 20 years. These resources, which come on stream from April 2001, will allow for the recruitment of hundreds more prosecutors and thousands more police and probation officers, as well as meeting a challenging list of Public Service Agreement (PSA) targets (see Annex C). But we will not get the full value of that investment if those new staff still have to operate within old systems and old ways of thinking, which stifle initiative and breed delay and inefficiency.

20   We must ensure that new investment leads to real change: real increases in the numbers of criminals convicted; real reductions in the number of crimes committed; real improvements in the confidence of victims and witnesses that justice is being delivered.

21   With the resources we have committed to tackling crime and reforming the CJS and through the major reforms outlined here, we aim to deliver by 2004:

- 100,000 more crimes where a victim sees an offender brought to justice;

- a 30 per cent reduction in vehicle crime; and a 25 per cent reduction in domestic burglary by 2005; and significant reductions in robbery in our principal cities – on track to meet our target of a 14 per cent reduction by 2005;

- a five per cent reduction in re-convictions by those under probation supervision – it is estimated that 200,000 crimes might be avoided each year through 30,000 offenders completing accredited programmes; and

- a 50 per cent increase in the number of qualifications achieved by prisoners in custody and double the number of prisoners going into jobs on their release.

22   How will all this be achieved? Our strategy has three core components.

23   First, a coordinated attack across Government on the causes of crime. Other departments including the Department for Education and Employment (DfEE), Department of Health (DH) and Department of the Environment, Transport and the Regions (DETR) are now spending billions each year on programmes which will have a direct impact in the short, medium and long term on crime rates: initiatives like Sure Start to improve the life chances of pre-school children; or the £600 million that DfEE is spending on tackling school truancy and exclusion; or the £900 million DETR is investing in turning around England's most deprived neighbourhoods, for whom high crime is one of the worst problems.

24   Second, a clear focus on the types of crime which most concern the public. By encouraging the police and local authorities to target domestic burglary and vehicle crime over the past four years we have made tremendous progress. Now we intend to apply that focused approach to other types of offence – in particular violent crime where we now have a clear strategy in place to make real inroads into offences like street robbery and alcohol related disorder.

25   Third, a comprehensive overhaul of the CJS to lever up performance in catching, trying, convicting, punishing and rehabilitating offenders.

26   Partly, this requires changes in process and method. But none of this will achieve its aim unless it is accompanied by a change in the culture of the whole system in which the particular responsibilities of each of the criminal justice professions are informed by the overriding social purpose of securing a more peaceful life for our citizens by delivering justice and reducing crime.

Introduction

27 This document focuses on the third element of this strategy – reform of the CJS. It draws on two key insights.

- first, that to get to grips with crime, we must get to grips with the 100,000 most persistent criminals who are estimated to commit half of all crime; and

- second, that as crime and criminality change, so too must the CJS.

28 By tackling both of these key challenges head on we aim to:

- close the 'justice gap' and bring more criminals to justice. By targeting persistent offenders and by investing in more staff and better skills, greater court and prison capacity and new technology we should catch and convict more persistent offenders, more often.

- ensure that punishments fit the criminal as well as the crime – with a clear message to all persistent offenders that they should reform or expect to stay under supervision. A new sentencing framework would ensure that short as well as long-term prisoners are supervised after release and by investing in drug treatment and more intensive support and surveillance for convicted offenders, we will get re-offending down.

- put the needs of victims and witnesses more at the centre, not at the periphery of the CJS. We propose new victims rights to ensure they get the service and support they deserve and we will make reporting crime and finding out about case progress much easier.

29 Getting crime down is central to the Government's vision of a society at one with itself, where all can prosper and everyone can enjoy reciprocal rights and responsibilities. Achieving such a vision however takes time; there is no quick fix.

30 We have made a good start – but there is much more to be done if we are to restore people's faith in the ability of the criminal system to deliver justice and help reduce crime. This document maps out the way ahead, a route map towards a safer society.

Executive Summary

1 The Government has embarked on a comprehensive, evidence-based programme to reduce crime, targeting both crime and its causes. This encompasses important programmes funded by the Department for Education and Employment, Department of Health and Department of the Environment, Transport and the Regions – initiatives like Sure Start for pre-school children and the Neighbourhood Renewal Strategy to turn around England's most deprived neighbourhoods.

2 The Government is also determined to build a CJS that is fair but effective, delivers swift justice, and deserves the full support and confidence of public and professionals alike. This document sets out what has already been achieved towards that goal, and the Government's strategy for the future.

Crime and the Criminal Justice System today

3 Although overall recorded crime is significantly higher than it was twenty or thirty years ago, the recent trend has been downwards, with particularly encouraging progress on property offences. Since 1997, overall crime has fallen by ten per cent with reductions of 21 per cent for domestic burglary and 15 per cent for vehicle crime.

4 Each day the police will handle over 25,500 '999' calls, make over 5,000 arrests and carry out 2,200 stop and searches. 4,400 jurors will be required to turn up for jury service, over 1,000 witnesses will attend court to give evidence and 5,600 defendants will be sentenced, of which 375 will enter prison.

5 To deal with this very considerable workload a complex range of local and national services and agencies has grown up. Over 300,000 people are dedicated to delivering results in the CJS, including police officers, prison and probation officers, barristers, solicitors, the judiciary and the magistracy, forensic scientists, and all of their support staff.

6 This is a huge investment of time, skill and resources and we must demand the best outcomes from it. But in spite of the skill and commitment of these people, the CJS's results are not always all that they should be. The public will judge the system by its performance in catching, convicting and punishing criminals. Over the last 20 years it has not kept pace both with the growth in crime, and new types of crime.

7 Far too few crimes are detected and prosecuted successfully. Cases still take too long and for too many persistent offenders, the system is a revolving door. Within two years of starting a community sentence, or finishing their prison sentence, over half of offenders will be back in court to be convicted and sentenced for further offences.

8 Unsurprisingly, this affects public confidence. Though witnesses at court generally feel satisfied with their treatment by the system (76 per cent) less than half of the public feel that the CJS is effective in bringing offenders to justice and only 26 per cent feel it meets the needs of victims.

Reducing crime and modernising the Criminal Justice System

9 Radical and systematic reform of the CJS has been a priority for the Government, starting with those parts of the CJS in most urgent need of change – the CPS and the youth justice system.

10 Now we are set on a wider programme of reform and investment for the whole CJS. This document takes forward the policies set out under the 2000 Spending Review, focusing in particular on:

- *catching and convicting more offenders* – so starting to increase the proportion of crimes reported to the police which end up with a criminal being brought to justice;

- *providing more resources than ever for the fight against drugs* to break the link between drugs and crime;

- *ensuring that punishments fit the criminal as well as the crime* to break cycles of repeat and persistent offending;

- *putting the needs of victims more at the centre* of the CJS to raise public confidence and ensure just outcomes for all;

- *supporting the police* in their twin aims of reducing crime and improving public reassurance;

- *combating international and organised crime* to make the UK one of the least attractive countries for organised criminal groups; and

- *joining it all up, securing better information and communications technology (ICT)*, promoting skills, equality and diversity within the CJS to improve its performance and the service it offers to the public.

Catching and convicting more offenders

11 We aim to enable the CJS to catch and convict more of the serious persistent offenders, more often. Using all the tools available – extra resources,

---

The biggest injection of new resources for the CJS in twenty years, an extra £1.4 billion in 2001-02 rising to £2.7 billion in 2003-04, will deliver ...

More staff:

- **An additional 9,000 police recruits over and above the number forces would otherwise have recruited over the period 2000-01 to 2002-03. By March 2003 police numbers should be at their highest ever level.**

- **Up to 700 new staff for the CPS by 2004, with a likely split of 300 lawyers and 400 caseworkers and administrative staff.**

Extra capacity:

- **7,000 extra Crown Court sitting days in 2001-02 with more to follow.**

- **Extra resources for magistrates' courts to cut delay and deal with more prosecutions.**

- **31 per cent increase in funding over 2001-02 to 2003-04 enabling the Probation Service to take on 1,450 new probation officers and 3,000 other staff.**

- **An extra 2,660 prison places and more investment in drug treatment in prison, offending behaviour programmes and basic skills training to help prisoners find work after release.**

Better information and communications technology:

- **By March 2002, every prison handling remand prisoners will have a video link to a magistrates' court.**

- **By 2003, all criminal justice professionals (police, probation, CPS, court clerks, prisons) will be able securely to e-mail each other.**

- **By 2004, an additional 2 million offenders will be on the DNA database and police officers on the beat will be able to transmit and receive photographs and Police National Computer data on-line via the Airwave service.**

Alongside new resources we will consider new procedures making it easier for courts to deliver justice, including:

- Simpler, fairer rules of evidence, so that magistrates and juries may have access to all the relevant and reliable material they need to acquit the innocent and convict the guilty.

- Better access by witnesses and jurors to written statements and interview transcripts and clearer rules on pre-trial disclosure of evidence by both sides.

- A new prosecution right of appeal against a range of judicial rulings, to reduce the number of cases which are dismissed prematurely.

- New laws to tackle offending on bail backed up by better information for courts.

- Reform of the criminal law to provide a consolidated, modernised core criminal code covering evidence, procedure, substantive offences and sentencing.

- More streamlined and effective court organisation and procedures, including links with the other criminal justice agencies.

Before decisions are made on these issues, the Government will consider carefully the recommendations of Sir Robin Auld's review of the criminal courts.

new technology and new techniques – the police will be able to give better priority to serious and persistent offenders. The whole active criminal population will be on the DNA database by 2004. The National Intelligence Model will be applied in every police force. There will be a CJS wide target to increase by 100,000 the number of recorded crimes ending in an offender being brought to justice.

12 We have substantially reformed the CPS by making its local boundaries coterminous with police areas, re-focusing it on its core business of prosecuting cases and enhancing local accountability. The reform process will continue, with the biggest

Drug related crime

- There will be more resources than ever before for the fight against drug related offending, including a 70 per cent increase over current spending levels on drug treatment services.

- We are already spending £60 million over 18 months for the Drug Treatment and Testing Order to be implemented nationally, to deliver an estimated 6,000 Orders saving up to 700,000 offences a year.

- By 2004, 25,000 prisoners will be going through the Prison Service drug programmes, with 5,700 of them going into intensive rehabilitation or therapeutic programmes.

- A new National Treatment Agency starting work this year will lever up the quality and availability of drug treatment.

- We will consider, with the police and other relevant agencies, the benefits of creating a register of drug dealers, similar to that which exists for sex offenders.

Executive Summary

injection of new resources since the CPS was founded, to provide more lawyers; improve prosecutors' skills; and provide a stronger role for the Chief Crown Prosecutors as local champions of justice, focused on key crimes and offenders.

Breaking the link between drugs and crime

13 Over the last four years, the Government has put in place the most ambitious anti-drugs strategy this country has ever seen. It is beginning to bite. Since 1997, the proportion of prisoners testing positive for drugs has fallen by a third and the first Drug Treatment and Testing Orders have resulted in significant reductions in drug related offending.

14 To break the links between drugs and crime, we aim to provide effective intervention at each stage of the criminal justice process – arrest, bail, sentencing, imprisonment and community supervision. We know treatment makes a difference. The key to success will be access to high quality treatment, therefore we are establishing a new National Treatment Agency.

Effective punishments to reduce re-offending

Young offenders

- **To break the links between school truancy and crime, police forces and education authorities will operate regular truancy sweeps and take tough action with persistent truants and their parents.**

- **We are investing £45 million over three years from April 2000 in a new Intensive Supervision and Surveillance Programme to deal with 2,500 of the most difficult and persistent young offenders.**

- **There will be 400 additional secure training centre places providing intensive supervision and high quality programmes for young people in custody.**

- **Every young offender in custody will get a minimum of 30 hours a week education, training or similar development work.**

Community punishments

- **A new National Probation Service will go live from April 2001 with a 31 per cent cash increase in funding over the next three years to deliver a five per cent reduction in reconvictions.**

Prison

- **An additional 2,660 prison places and 400 new places in secure training centres for young offenders.**

- **More money for regimes to increase to nearly 9,000 the number of prisoners completing accredited offending behaviour programmes and to provide a 50 per cent increase in the number of qualifications gained by prisoners.**

- **A new £30 million Custody to Work programme to double by 2004 the number of prisoners going into jobs when they leave prison.**

- **More effective reintegration from custody into the community, possibly best achieved through a new 'Custody Plus' sentence.**

Punishments that fit the criminal as well as the crime

15 Within two years of starting a community sentence, or finishing their prison sentence, over half of offenders – and nearly 80 per cent of those with more than five previous convictions – will be back in court to be convicted and sentenced for further offences.

16 Too often, short sentence prisoners leave custody just as illiterate, as unemployable and as prone to drug dependence as when they went in. And under the current sentencing framework, short term prisoners know that there will be no follow up supervision to keep them away from crime after their release. This is unacceptable, which is why the Government commissioned a major review of the sentencing framework, expected to report in May 2001[1].

17 The Government aims to establish a new sentencing framework, focused on crime reduction as well as punishment for the immediate crime, which ensures greater consistency and that persistent offending leads to increased severity of punishment. There will be much greater post-release supervision of short sentence prisoners and a new emphasis on on-going sentence management and review.

Meeting the needs of victims and witnesses

18 When a crime is committed, victims need the CJS to deliver justice, protection and service. Victims also want to put the crime behind them and get on with the rest of their lives.

19 Support for victims in the UK is already high by international standards and we have the most generous Criminal Injuries Compensation Scheme in the world. But the Government is determined to do still more to deliver a better deal for victims and witnesses – including the large number of victims whose crime is never solved and who do not have the satisfaction of seeing an offender brought to justice.

20 At the heart of our new deal for victims will be a new Charter of Rights setting out clear standards of service as to how every victim should be treated. Where the service received falls short of those standards there will be a Victims' Ombudsman to put matters right.

Placing victims more at the heart of the Criminal Justice System

We will make sure that:

- **Victims are kept properly informed throughout the progress of their case.**

- **From October 2001, all victims will be able to submit a 'victim personal statement' to the courts and other criminal justice agencies setting out the effect of the crime on their lives.**

- **By 2005, victims will begin to be able to track the progress of their case online.**

- **From April this year, every victim of a violent or sex offence will be consulted and notified about relevant release conditions when an offender sentenced to more than 12 months in prison is to be released.**

- **And by the end of 2001, victims will be able to report non-urgent minor crimes to the police online via the Internet.**

Executive Summary

A modern police service

The Government will be supporting the police through:

- **A 21 per cent cash increase in police funding over the period 2000-01 to 2003-04, including £500 million to fund Airwave – a new national secure digital radio system.**

- **Funding for an additional 9,000 recruits over and above what forces would otherwise have recruited over the period 2000-01 to 2002-03, which should take overall police numbers to their highest ever level by March 2003.**

- **An increase in trained detective capability including, where necessary, opportunities to recruit people with relevant specialist skills from other fields.**

- **An expansion of the DNA database to cover the whole active criminal population by April 2004.**

- **Experimental accreditation of security or patrol staff from other organisations, working under police co-ordination to deliver improved community safety.**

Helping the police to reduce crime and increase public reassurance

21 The Government has been working with the police and HM Inspectorate of Constabulary on a programme of reforms to raise police performance in reducing crime and increasing public reassurance. Some elements of the reform programme are underway already, with legislation before Parliament; other parts will need considerable development work and discussion before they can be finalised; and some ideas are clearly experimental and will have to be judged on the results of carefully evaluated trials.

Combating organised crime

We will:

- **Introduce new legislation – the Proceeds of Crime Bill – to tackle money laundering and introduce new powers to strengthen the law on asset seizure.**

- **Develop better procedures for co-ordinating and analysing intelligence through adoption of the National Intelligence Model and develop a new National Hi-Tech Crime Strategy.**

- **Strengthen international co-operation to tackle more effectively cross-border crime and improve extradition procedures.**

- **Develop stronger links between specialist prosecutors and joint training for investigators by a new Specialist Law Enforcement Centre.**

- **Examine the case for reforming the law to deal with new and increasingly sophisticated forms of organised crime.**

Combating organised crime

22 Whether involved in drug trafficking, major fraud or laundering money, organised groups increasingly operate on a global scale, using sophisticated techniques to secure huge profits. Just a few organised individuals hold criminal assets worth millions of pounds. We therefore need to develop equally sophisticated methods to prevent and tackle organised crime by disrupting criminal networks, seizing their assets and bringing organised criminals to justice.

Joining it all up

23 To reduce crime effectively, to deliver justice and to enhance public confidence, the CJS has to work as a coherent, joined-up system, with all those involved adopting a common set of values to meet a common set of goals. To achieve this, we will:

- set a clear performance management framework, with a small number of simple targets, clear accountability, effective incentives and support for managers;

- join up criminal justice agencies locally and nationally, ensuring they have strong links to Crime and Disorder Reduction and Local Strategic Partnerships and are ready to listen to and learn from their local communities;

- endeavour to build a highly skilled, highly motivated workforce, representative of the communities it serves, with shared aims, shared values and shared outcomes; and

- consult on a draft set of core principles for the CJS, to recognise and underpin its public service ethos.

24 Improving the performance of the CJS also means giving practitioners the tools they need to do the job. Almost £1 billion will be invested in ICT over the next ten years to transform the way the system collects, uses and exchanges information in order to raise performance and provide a better service to the public. We aim to ensure those who use the system – victims, witnesses, jurors – as well as practitioners, will have the information they need, when they need it, in a simple and easily accessible form. By 2005, criminal justice organisations (police, probation, CPS, courts, prisons) should be able to exchange case file information electronically.

Possibilities for joining up the Criminal Justice System

- **Establishing a strengthened Strategic Planning Board to provide a clear strategic direction, take more account of the views of practitioners and maximise the capacity of managers to deliver on the ground.**

- **Developing effective incentives for improved performance by rewarding success.**

- **Co-ordination of inspection programmes, with more cross-cutting, 'thematic' inspections.**

- **New structures to drive up performance and standards across the system.**

Before decisions are made on these issues, the Government will consider carefully the recommendations of Sir Robin Auld's review of the criminal courts.

Executive Summary

The way ahead

25 Lessons from the transformation of the youth justice system since 1997 show that new resources, structures and powers are important. But almost more important is securing a changed philosophy and the shared duty on everyone working in the youth justice system to deliver an outcome – less offending and re-offending.

- *Part 1* of this document reviews the current performance of the CJS and draws conclusions for better targeting its efforts – on persistent offenders, on types of crime, and on high crime areas;

- *Part 2* sets out the work in hand and for the future in preventing and addressing offending; and

- *Part 3* sets out work in hand and possible future developments to draw on the lessons of the last four years to modernise the CJS in its entirety.

26 The proposals set out here will build on the foundation laid in the 2000 Spending Review, which set demanding targets and objectives through Public Service Agreements for:

- the Criminal Justice System as a whole;

- Action Against Illegal Drugs; and

- crime reduction, through targets in individual Departments' PSAs.

Feedback

27 The recommendations of Sir Robin Auld's review of the criminal courts, and of the Sentencing Review, will be based on extensive consultation and will drive further considerations of much of the reform programme set out in this document. In addition the Government will, as indicated in the text, consult specifically over the way particular strands of the programme are to be taken forward.

28 Any comments of a general nature on the content of this document may be sent to:

Home Office, Room 365,
50 Queen Anne's Gate,
London SW1H 9AT.

Part 1
Analysis and basic conclusions

The state of the Criminal Justice System today

1.1 The Government has made considerable strides in reducing crime. Overall crime is down by ten per cent since 1997, and vehicle crime and burglary by significantly more (15 per cent and 21 per cent respectively).[1] Clear crime reduction strategies backed with significant new resources are now in place at local and national level. Everyone working in the police service and across the CJS can be proud of this record.

1.2 This work has been part of a far-reaching programme of reform and modernisation of the CJS. Four years ago, the system was under-resourced and under-performing. So, with practioners, the Government embarked first on reform of the two crucial parts of the system in most urgent need of attention – the CPS and the youth justice system.[2]

1.3 Following the Glidewell Review,[3] the CPS has now been reorganised so that its boundaries are coterminous with those of the police, with a Chief Crown Prosecutor in each area. Compared with our European neighbours, the number of prosecutors per capita in England and Wales is low.[4] CPS resources next year are to be increased by 23 per cent in real terms to build on the reforms already underway.

1.4 Meanwhile we are transforming the youth justice system, concentrating minds and efforts across different agencies on the single aim of preventing offending. Police, social services, probation, education and health are now working together in Youth Offending Teams to provide effective, early intervention to prevent offending, as well as programmes that tackle the causes of offending.

Courts are able to ensure parents of young offenders face their responsibilities and receive help with parenting. Young offenders are now confronted with their responsibility for their crime; where they want to, victims are becoming involved through reparation and restorative justice. We have also made good progress in speeding up youth justice: the average time taken to deal with persistent young offenders has fallen by a third.[5]

1.5 We have also established 376 Crime and Disorder Reduction Partnerships across England and Wales. These bring together local authorities, police, and a wide range of other local agencies, with a statutory duty[6] to devise and implement crime reduction strategies for their areas. Authorities are required to take crime reduction into account in the way they exercise all their functions. This document is principally concerned with the functioning of the CJS, from the point at which an offence is reported to the police, but other local agencies working in partnership with the police are an increasingly important means of preventing crime occurring and of building up a sense of community safety.

1.6 We have also set about rebuilding the confidence of the public in the CJS, for it cannot function effectively without their support. We have given strong support to the Neighbourhood Watch movement, which now has 160,000 separate local schemes involving over six million households. Funding for Victim Support has doubled since 1997, not least so that they can run a Witness Service in every magistrates' court as well as the Crown Court.

1.7 Since 1997, the Government has also set out – for the first time – overarching aims, objectives and targets for the CJS as a whole. We are beginning to

[1] *The 2000 British Crime Survey* (2000).
[2] *Misspent Youth: Young People and Crime* (1996).
[3] *Review of the Crown Prosecution Service* (1998).
[4] Using data from the *Fifth UN Survey of Crime Trends and the Operation of the Criminal Justice System*, the average number of prosecutors per 100,000 in 1994 was: Portugal (10), Belgium and Sweden (8), Denmark, Finland and Germany (7), Scotland (5), England and Wales (4) and Spain and the Netherlands (3). Data for the USA is also presented (9). These figures give only an indication of country differences since the definition of prosecutors differs across countries.
[5] *Statistics on Persistent Young Offenders* (2001).
[6] Under the Crime and Disorder Act 1998.

make the CJS work as a *system*: local agency boundaries are now coterminous and we have established joined-up planning and management at national level.

1.8 This reform is unfolding in tandem with significant investment. Over the next three years, investment in policing and crime fighting will rise by more than 20 per cent in cash terms – almost 11 per cent in real terms. Police funding will increase by 21 per cent over three years 2001-2004. £1.7 billion has been allocated for expenditure on the criminal courts in 2001-02 and investment in the CPS will rise by almost a quarter in real terms.

1.9 The Government wants to consider fully and carefully the scope for moving to a more streamlined criminal court system, reducing paperwork and speeding up justice, and operating closely with the other criminal justice agencies. We also want to consider a radical overhaul of rules of evidence and codification of the criminal law, criminal procedure and rules of evidence.

1.10 In order to be able to do this with the best considered advice, at the end of 1999 the Government asked Sir Robin Auld, a highly experienced Lord Justice of Appeal, to conduct a comprehensive and independent review of the criminal courts.[7] Sir Robin Auld's review has been open – with widespread consultation, seminars and the use of a website[8] to issue information on progress. He has received submissions of evidence from about 1,000 persons and organisations.

1.11 The issues Sir Robin Auld is considering are complex and interlocking. Once his report is received by Government, we will consult appropriately on his findings before providing a detailed response. Depending on when the review is completed,

we hope that a detailed response may be made through a White Paper before the end of 2001.

1.12 Sir Robin Auld's recommendations will inform all decisions taken to develop the CJS, particularly in regard to law reform, rules of evidence, courts and the trial process, but also in regard to many aspects of the treatment of victims, the strategic direction of the CJS, and the development of information and communications technology (ICT) on a CJS wide basis. The Government wants follow-up to Sir Robin Auld's review to replicate in the criminal courts the success of the reform process undertaken following Lord Woolf's review of the civil justice system.[9]

1.13 Why the urgency and the scale of reform? Despite our successes to date, crime is still far higher now than it was 20 or 30 years ago. There are many reasons for this – including changing attitudes towards wrong-doing, a huge increase in the number of attractive, stealable possessions and increasing hard drug use. But one important underlying factor is that the CJS has not been effective enough in dealing with crime or offenders.

1.14 Over the last 20 years, despite the efforts of thousands of skilled and dedicated police and CJS practitioners, which has produced marked reductions in some offences, the system has not kept pace with the growth in crime nor with new types of crime and criminality.

1.15 Too few crimes are detected and prosecuted successfully and police clear-up rates have fallen – from 40 per cent in 1980 to 24 per cent today on a like-for-like basis. This should be tempered by the fact that the police have had to face a substantial increase in workload – recorded crime rose by around

---

[7] The terms of reference are: To review the practices and procedures of, and the rules of evidence applied by, the criminal courts at every level, with a view to ensuring that they deliver justice fairly, by streamlining all their processes, increasing their efficiency and strengthening the effectiveness of their relationships with others across the whole of the criminal justice system, and having regard to the interests of all parties including victims and witnesses, thereby promoting public confidence in the rule of law.

[8] www.criminal-courts-review.org.uk

[9] Lord Woolf's Review reported on 28 July 1996.

three quarters during this period – however the proportion of crimes which result in a conviction has also fallen.

1.16 Cases still take too long. Sentencing is both too variable and insufficiently focused on reducing re-offending. For too many persistent offenders, the system is a revolving door: their repeated trips to court and spells in prison fail to change their attitudes or address the underlying causes of their offending behaviour and thus do little to stop them offending again.

1.17 The system's failure to keep pace with crime results in part from inadequate capital investment. For example, staff in some agencies have been struggling without access to the most basic information technology. Up to November 2000, fewer than one in five CPS lawyers and caseworkers had access to a computer. And the justice system's failure to adopt the standard working tools and practices of the day is symptomatic of a deeper failure to modernise and to connect with the citizens it is supposed to serve.

1.18 While practitioners within the CJS are highly skilled and committed, the CJS as a system is poorly understood by the public at large. Not least, this is because its rules and procedures are complex, often highly technical and sometimes perceived as archaic. Whilst the majority of the public (over two thirds) are confident that the system operates fairly for the defendant, only half believe that it is effective in bringing offenders to justice and even fewer – about a quarter – believe it meets the needs of victims.[10] Those with recent experience of the courts as victims and/or witnesses are more

confident in the system, with four out of five witnesses believing that it treats defendants fairly.[11]

1.19 We also know that the CJS impacts disproportionately on those from minority ethnic communities, who are not only more likely to be victims of crime,[12] but are also more likely to be caught up in the CJS. Black people are five times more likely to be stopped and searched by police than white people. They are also four times more likely to be arrested and once convicted, tend to receive longer custodial sentences.[13] Members of minority ethnic communities, and black people in particular, are far less confident than white members of the public that defendants are fairly treated by the system.[14]

1.20 These challenges are augmented by the simple fact that crime is ever changing. Criminality reflects the society that spawns it – and so crime, like society, is now changing more rapidly than ever.

1.21 For example, new technology brings with it the potential for new types of offending which we could never have guessed at a generation ago – such as Internet pornography, computer hacking or the theft of digital services. A recent report[15] has identified further likely developments over the next twenty years, providing a glimpse of new kinds of crime that will emerge and how we might begin to tackle them (see Annex G). New consumer products bring huge benefits but also potential crime epidemics. At least one in three street robberies in London now involves a mobile phone.[16] Credit card fraud more than doubled between 1995 and 1999 from £83.3 million to £189.3 million.[17]

---

[10] *Confidence in the Criminal Justice System: Findings from the 2000 British Crime Survey* (2001).

[11] *Key findings from the Witness Satisfaction Survey 2000* (forthcoming).

[12] *Ethnicity and Victimisation: Findings from the 1996 BCS* (1998).

[13] *Statistics on Race and the Criminal Justice System: A Home Office publication under section 95 of the Criminal Justice Act 1991* (2000).

[14] 52 per cent of black people and 66 per cent of Asian people are confident the system respects the rights of people accused of committing a crime and treats them fairly, compared to 70 per cent of white people. *Confidence in the Criminal Justice System: Findings from the 2000 British Crime Survey* (2001).

[15] *Turning the Corner* (2000)

[16] Figures provided by the Metropolitan Police Force (unpublished).

[17] *The Economic Cost of Fraud* (2000).

Analysis and basic conclusions

1.22 New leisure patterns also make a difference. The boom in the night-time leisure economy has transformed many of our city centres. This has been good for the economy as a whole: one in five new jobs are now being created in restaurants, clubs or other licensed premises. But it has brought problems too. In 1999, victims in 53 per cent of stranger violence incidents judged their attackers to be under the influence of alcohol. Pubs and clubs are the third most common location for violence, after the home and the street.[18]

1.23 The use of hard drugs has greatly increased. It is estimated that two thirds of persistent offenders use hard drugs. Property crime is fuelled by drug misuse to a far greater extent now than 30 years ago.[19]

1.24 Finally, in a more and more globalised environment, crime increasingly crosses international borders. As well as the international trade in illegal drugs, we are now faced with a massive trade in 'bootleg' tobacco and alcohol, and a £500 million[20] illegal immigration business. Crimes committed in one jurisdiction may involve criminals in an entirely different one. To bring multi-national criminal gangs to justice may involve several trials in many different countries, each with their own criminal procedures and rules of evidence. And tracking down and confiscating criminal assets sometimes worth hundreds of millions of pounds presents huge challenges to law enforcement.

1.25 The CJS must keep pace with such changes. This is the broader challenge of modernisation. It will take concerted effort. Much of our criminal law remains rooted in the nineteenth century. The criminal courts system has evolved piecemeal. The origins of some of our rules of evidence are to be found in a different age when the spoken not the written word was the primary form of communication, when jury members could not always be assumed to be able to read or write, and when defendants were rarely legally represented.

1.26 But the need to modernise goes beyond the court system. Other parts of the CJS have suffered too from inadequate or fragmented patterns of investment. It might have made sense 30 years ago for each of our 43 police forces to have its own radio communications system. It makes no sense at all now.

1.27 The Government is determined to modernise the CJS so that it is able to keep pace with changing patterns of crime, and so that it can drive down crime. In particular, the CJS now needs to build on the successes of the last four years by better targeting its efforts. We must:

- catch and convict more of the hard core of persistent offenders, more often, and deal with them more quickly;

- provide tough, effective punishments that become progressively more intense for persistent offenders and that work to reduce their re-offending; and

- tackle the underlying causes of crime and intervene early with those young people most at risk of developing into the next generation of high rate offenders.

Who? Targeting offenders

1.28 Recent research suggests that a small group of hard core, highly persistent offenders, probably no more than 100,000 strong – about ten per cent of all active criminals – may be responsible for *half* of all crime.

---

[18] Tables A2.9 and A6.11, *The 2000 British Crime Survey* (2000).
[19] *Digest 4: Information on the criminal justice system in England and Wales* (1999).
[20] 1998 figure.

- *Providing greater openness and accountability* – virtually all judicial vacancies – all but the most senior – are now filled through open competition.[110] A Judicial Appointments Commissioner[111] is being established to monitor judicial appointment procedures.

- *Looking after victims and witnesses* – with dedicated Witness Services being established in all courts.

- *Delivering better ICT* – including a large programme for the computerisation of magistrates' courts to be rolled out from the second half of 2001.

3.64 The Government's proposals to give the courts, rather than the defendant, the power to decide whether a triable either way case would be heard in the Crown Court will build on these achievements. These proposals aim to speed up justice and help victims and witnesses, whilst ensuring that defendants receive a fair trial.

We are investing for continued reform and improvement

3.65 The necessary resources have been committed following the 2000 Spending Review – £1.7 billion has been allocated for expenditure on the criminal courts in 2001-02. This includes some £40 million that criminal justice Ministers allocated in December 2000 from the joint CJS Reserve to fund, amongst other initiatives, an extra 7,000 Crown Court sitting days in 2001-02 and work in the magistrates' courts on initiatives to speed up youth justice and prosecute more defendants.

Should our court structure be changed?

3.66 We also need to ensure that we have the right structure and approach. At the moment, we have two largely separate criminal court systems. The great bulk of criminal business (about 95 per cent) is dealt with in the magistrates' courts by magistrates and District Judges. The magistrates' courts aim to deliver local and summary justice; their jurisdiction is generally limited to offences committed in their immediate area. The most serious 5 per cent of cases are dealt with at Crown Court centres by judges and juries. The Crown Court has a national jurisdiction as part of the Supreme Court.

3.67 The administration of the two court systems is completely different. Magistrates' courts are administered by local MCCs, largely made up of local magistrates. Local Authorities meet 20 per cent of their administration costs; the Lord Chancellor's Department (LCD) meets the other 80 per cent. Magistrates' courts buildings are owned or leased by local authorities. The Crown Court is administered by the Court Service, an agency of the LCD. The Crown Court estate is managed by the LCD on behalf of the Crown.

A unified court structure?

3.68 Evidence put to Sir Robin Auld has suggested a case for unifying the magistrates' courts and Crown Court. A common jurisdiction, procedures and processes, and common administration might:

- Reduce the complexity of the criminal system, facilitating swifter justice.

- Enable greater flexibility in the distribution of work, increasing efficiency.

- Streamline the system.

---

[110]In 1999-2000 some 4,000 judicial vacancies were filled by open competition as against 3 senior appointments from the High Court to the Court of Appeal Cm 4783, October 2000. Not all solely criminal appointments – the 4,000 includes tribunal, recorders, Circuit and District Judges and High Court judges.

[111]Recommendation of Sir Leonard Peach's report December 1999 on appointment and selection procedures.

3.69 Sir Robin Auld's recommendations on this will be considered carefully, in consultation with the judiciary, the magistracy, court staff, and the legal professions, as well as those representing the police, CPS, and wider interests of victims and the public.

3.70 A central question would be how to *manage* any unified court system. This would not necessarily require a single court agency: other models exist, including retaining a significant element of local control and accountability, aligned to the 42 CPS/police force areas. The Government would also want to examine the exact mechanisms for inspection and local accountability of any unified structure.

3.71 Patterns of crime and criminality are changing and the courts need to be equipped to respond effectively. The scope for specialist hearings dealing for example with drugs offences or domestic violence will also be considered in this context.

3.72 Specialist expertise is particularly important in the area of serious and organised crime (for example drug trafficking, serious sexual assault and homicide). Training for the judiciary and magistracy in complex cases will continue, ensuring that only those who have received proper and up to the minute training deal with such cases.

3.73 There have also been suggestions made to Sir Robin Auld that some court business should be handled through an 'immediate tier' of courts where a District Judge would sit with two lay magistrates, and on the use of juries in complex cases. The Government will give any recommendations he makes on these issues careful consideration, and open them to wide consultation before embarking on any implementation.

We will continue to reduce delay

3.74 Delay in court processes is in no one's interests. Following the publication in 1997 of the 'Narey Report' into reducing delay,[112] the Government responded quickly by piloting measures to speed up the progress of criminal cases. These measures were adopted nationally from November 1999, with the co-operation of the police, CPS, magistrates' courts, Crown Court, Home Office, LCD and the Attorney General's Office, and are having tangible results:

- *Early First Hearings* mean that offenders who plead guilty are now dealt with only a few days after charge.

- *Criminal Justice Units*, bringing together CPS and police to prepare case files, have improved efficiency and effectiveness; and some 190 CPS staff have been specially trained as 'Designated Caseworkers' to review and present cases in court.

- *Indictable only* cases now bypass traditional committal proceedings and go straight from an initial hearing to the Crown Court.[113]

- *Statutory time limits* are being piloted in selected youth courts.

3.75 These measures have demonstrated the capacity for high levels of co-operative working in the CJS – and the rewards it can bring. The challenge now is to extend to a wider group of defendants, such as those charged for summary offences, our success in getting cases into court quickly and dealing with persistent young offenders.

---

[112]*Review of Delay in the Criminal Justice System* (1997).
[113]Implemented across England and Wales 15 January 2001.

3.76 We need to reduce waiting times for trials and committals in both the magistrates' court and the Crown Court. New investment will help. The CPS will be able to prepare cases quicker and better. The enhanced professionalism brought about by the Criminal Defence Service (CDS – see below) will see an end to time wasting and poor preparation. Case progression officers have been appointed in every Crown Court centre and we have allocated £4 million from the CJS reserve for similar arrangements in magistrates' courts. Simple, practical innovations can yield substantial gains (see box)

control in the current criminal legal aid system. The CDS will play its part in responding to any recommendations from Sir Robin Auld on pre-trial case management.

3.79 Under the CDS, aided representation will be available without regard to a defendant's means. But those accused of certain crimes (such as drug trafficking, serious fraud or money laundering), as well as those who are personally wealthy, will be the subject of detailed investigation to establish whether they can afford to pay towards the cost of

Hampshire youth courts

In Southampton, the youth court used to sit every weekday. Like most courts, it was plagued by cases which had to be adjourned. So they re-organised sittings so that an additional youth court sat three days a week. They were able to list more cases. A District Judge reviewed all the cases for the day first thing in the morning, adjourned those which could not proceed and released the remaining trials to the other courts.

They cut their waiting times for trials from 13 weeks to just under four weeks.

A new Criminal Defence Service

3.77 We cannot achieve our aim of a fair, effective CJS without a high quality, cost effective, publicly funded legal defence service. Defendants need to have the confidence that they will be acquitted, if innocent. Equally those who are guilty should feel they will be fairly treated if they plead guilty. If defendants lack confidence in the basic fairness of the system, they may attempt to frustrate it, leading to increased legal argument, delay, cost, and anxiety for victims.

3.78 From April 2001 the new CDS will provide advice, assistance and representation for defendants by contracted, quality assured criminal practitioners. A salaried defence service will also be established, to provide greater choice of representatives for defendants and more flexibility in meeting demand. These changes should improve quality and cost

their defence. At the end of every Crown Court trial the judge will consider whether an individual can afford to pay for their defence and whether they should in fact be ordered to do so.

We will bring courts closer to the people they serve

3.80 The Government wants to see strong links not only between the courts and their criminal justice partners at local level but also between the courts and local residents. People should look upon their local magistrates' or Crown Court as a public service in the same way they view hospitals or schools.

Modernising the Criminal Justice System

Community involvement – magistrates

The lay magistracy is one of the largest voluntary groups in the CJS with over 30,000 people giving up their time to train and to sit on the Bench. It is not an easy task and the Government values the important work they do. The pre-eminent requirement is that a candidate must be personally suitable for appointment, but strenuous efforts are made to ensure that each lay bench broadly reflects the community it serves, in terms of gender, ethnic origin and geographical spread.

Recent research[114] has confirmed that those efforts have achieved a balance of men and women and that "the composition of the lay magistracy nationally is now approaching ethnic representativeness."

There are still variations locally in ethnic composition of the lay bench in relation to the local population. There is also often an imbalance of age range. The Lord Chancellor is addressing these concerns by commissioning a National Strategy for the Recruitment of Lay Magistrates.

3.81 In the youth justice system, innovative Youth Offender Panels[115] are bringing local residents, young offenders and families together to negotiate the substance of referral orders – appropriate punishments which make reparation to victims and address the causes of the offending. These Panels are chaired by a local person, and demonstrate the scope for greater community involvement in our system of justice.

Making better use of court houses

3.82 Most magistrates' courts in England and Wales sit every weekday, morning and afternoon. Additionally, out of hours arrangements exist enabling agencies to call upon the services of magistrates and legal advisers and to arrange emergency applications and court hearings. Courts also sit on Saturdays and Bank Holidays to deal with those arrested and detained by the police.

3.83 It has been suggested that courts in England and Wales should open longer, to improve the service they give to the public and to cut delays. In crime hotspots, courts could sit late and at the weekend if this would have an impact on delays, deter local

criminals, and help to reassure local communities. We will pilot an initiative to find the most cost-effective means of extending court hours with these aims. The pilot would need to ensure that all relevant agencies are geared up to work and cooperate during the extended hours, and would examine issues such as:

- what type of work should be dealt with during non-core working hours?

- what is the impact of extended court hours on productivity, case progression and the speed of justice?

- what are the costs and benefits for victims, witnesses and other members of the public who might be attending court during extended hours? What is the effect on public confidence?

3.84 In addition, we want to assess the costs and benefits of extended sitting hours for magistrates' courts in non-high crime areas. A second pilot will take place in 2001 that will involve the courts sitting into the evening and court staff providing an information service beyond the usual office hours.

---

[114]*The Judiciary in the Magistrates' Courts* (2000)
[115]Established under the Youth Justice and Criminal Evidence Act 1999.

More information for the public

3.85 Findings from the People's Panel[116] show a public appetite for more information about court business. Each MCC now publishes the performance standards to which it must work and an Annual Report setting out achievements. But more is needed. The public should be able to obtain at any time information about, for example, the dates of future hearings. Victims, in particular, have a legitimate interest in greater information. By 2005, we will be introducing online case listing and case results for all courts, so any member of the public can find out basic information.

3.86 The internet should be fully exploited. Some magistrates' courts, such as Swansea and Bedfordshire, have already set up their own web-sites. But sometimes members of the public want and need to talk to court staff out of hours (see box).

Out of hours information service

An out of hours information service will be piloted in magistrates' courts in 2001. Furthermore the Crown Court Programme includes the provision of better information for court users, outside normal business hours, via online information.

3.87 These developments will parallel those for civil courts, described in the 'Modernising the Civil Courts' consultation paper.[117] If these pilots are successful we will have better use of court premises, better services to the public and better access to information and help.

More to increase public understanding

3.88 In many parts of the country, the courts are already taking initiatives to increase public understanding of their work. The Lord Chief Justice has encouraged judges to visit schools to talk about their work. The Magistrates' Association runs a successful community programme, funded by the LCD. Open days and mock trials competitions are already an established feature for both magistrates' and the Crown Court.

The Crown Court at Shrewsbury

Shrewsbury Crown Court worked with local practitioners and BBC Radio Shropshire to produce a series of programmes based on a mock trial – after which members of the public were invited to phone in to discuss issues raised, and to find out more about the CJS.

3.89 In addition, the *'Just Ask!'* website[118] of the Community Legal Service will carry a wide range of educational material on both the civil and criminal judicial processes. It will show how a hypothetical case progresses from arrest to sentence.

3.90 The Government will ensure that court staff in each of the 42 criminal justice areas have the responsibility, with the judiciary, to improve relations with local people and their understanding of the criminal courts. The courts must be better able to respond to the increasingly diverse range of people using them and to recognise their differing needs.

---

[116]This is a panel of 5,000 members of the public randomly selected by MORI from across the UK who are representative of the whole UK population. The panel is used to test reaction to Government modernisation issues.

[117]*Modernising the Civil Courts – A Consultation Paper* (2001).

[118]www.justask.org.uk

Modernising the Criminal Justice System

3.91 Public understanding and accountability could be further enhanced by making available comparative statistics on court use and cost per sitting hour, bearing in mind the need to reflect differences in caseload between courts. The public is also entitled to be able to assess the consistency of judicial decision-making. We shall work up ways of presenting reliable comparative information, also including for example the percentage of breaches of bail conditions, percentage of committals outstanding over 16 weeks and days on which juries hear cases as a percentage of attendance.

3.92 The Government does not favour the televising of trials. We believe that this would distort the trial process and be unfair to witnesses and jurors. However we do believe that there is a case for the public to be able to watch appeal proceedings via television. Within the existing law, we will consider requests by television companies who may be interested in making a pilot to demonstrate to the Lord Chancellor and to the senior judiciary the potential educational benefits of such a programme.

The public has an important role to play through jury service

3.93 The public has a right to expect a criminal court system that is fair, effective and connected to local people. Members of the public also have a responsibility to play their part within that system, through jury service.

3.94 To be properly effective, the Government believes that juries need to reflect the communities from which they are drawn. Recent research into excusals from jury service suggests that less than half of those summoned for jury service actually serve.[119]

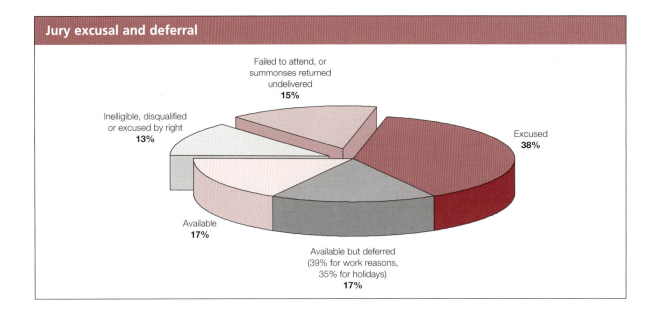

Jury excusal and deferral

Failed to attend, or summonses returned undelivered
15%

Inelligible, disqualified or excused by right
13%

Excused
38%

Available
17%

Available but deferred
(39% for work reasons, 35% for holidays)
17%

[119]*Jury excusal and deferral* (1999).

Modernisation in practice – The Crown Court Programme

This programme will test and develop ways of providing a radically better service to the public, particularly victims and witnesses. It has been designed with the help of the judiciary and criminal justice organisations and is being funded with £32 million from the Capital Modernisation Fund and £62 million from Spending Review 2000.

Through six major projects, it will:

- Help meet the requirement for electronic delivery of services by 2005 – using e-mail, strategic system to system links, and web-based information.

- Help meet the requirement for electronic storage of public records by 2004.

- Work towards the development of a single CJS electronic case file.

Specific improvements should include:

- Saving time and paperwork by using evidence in electronic format and electronic case listing.

- Sharing information across the CJS, eg immediate notification of sentences to the prison or probation services.

- Providing better information for court users outside normal court hours, via kiosks, electronic noticeboards and online information.

- Providing better case management, with case progression officers in all court centres and more flexible handling of PDHs, dealing with issues online.

The Crown Court at Kingston is being developed as a 'pathfinder' – it will be fully functioning by the end of March 2001. Pilots will then start later in 2001 and, subject to successful evaluation, roll-out to all court centres will be between 2001 and 2004.

Specific achievements so far include:

- *JUROR* – a centralised juror summonsing process, delivering faster, electronic payments to jurors. This service could be extended to enable web-based services – eg for jurors to complete and return forms online.

- *For victims and witnesses* – an additional 70 sets of CCTV kit, at a cost of £800,000 per year for the next nine years is being provided to enable more victims and witnesses to give evidence remotely, reducing their stress and anxiety.

- Judicial Technology – to supply all full-time judges in England and Wales with ICT to assist them in court and in chambers. Over 1,000 judges have had training and workstations so far – providing standard office applications, specialised email and conferencing facilities and full internet access. Further training and supply of workstations is being arranged for 200 more judges between March and June 2001.

Modernisation in practice – the Crown Court Programme (cont)

- Through the internet, all users can access *Lexicon*, a website maintained by the Court Service providing access to Human Rights websites, the All England Law Reports and Butterworth's statute law database. A customised 'alerter' service will keep judges up to date with developments in the field(s) of law in which they are interested.

Modernisation in practice – The Magistrates' Courts ICT Programme

The programme, known as Libra, will deliver new ICT services to the magistrates' courts and provide electronic links to all agencies in the criminal justice system.

- The project will:

  - deliver a national infrastructure across the courts by the summer of 2002

  - develop and deliver a new application to replace the ageing systems currently in the courts, to be completed in 2003.

- The service will provide magistrates' courts with modern tools to improve their administrative processes, including in-court computing.

- The infrastructure will provide the basis for the development of electronic services to the public and professions, including listing and results information. These services will be introduced progressively and will be complete by 2005.

- Electronic links with other agencies will be implemented as each new system in the other agencies comes on stream.

A better deal for victims and witnesses

Delivery timetable

- From April 2001 – Probation Service duty to keep victims of serious violent and sexual crimes informed of offender's release and conditions;

- October 2001 – victim personal statements introduced;

- By March 2002 – Witness Service established in every magistrates' court; and

- By October 2002 – CPS programme for direct communication with victims implemented.

Key measures

- Consultation on a new Victim's Charter from February 2001 (including whether to establish statutory rights and a Victims' Ombudsman) with a view to implementing a revised Charter by November 2001.

- A duty to be placed on the Probation Service to keep victims of serious violent and sexual crimes informed of offender's release and conditions from April 2001.

- Victim personal statements setting out to the police how the crime has affected their lives to be introduced from October 2001.

- A Witness Service in every magistrates' court by March 2002.

- The implementation of a CPS programme to inform victims in writing about key casework decisions by October 2002.

- Improvements in court facilities to ensure the separation of prosecution witnesses from potentially intimidating witnesses and their families.

- A 30 per cent increase in funding for Victim Support for 2001-02 and the possible introduction of a Victim's Fund to ensure victims receive immediate compensation.

- Increases in compensation for victims of rape and child abuse and for bereaved partners in fatal cases.

- More help to reduce repeat victimisation.

- Better standards of service for victims, with more information and greater convenience, including the extension of UKOnline service to facilitate the reporting of minor crimes.

Modernising the Criminal Justice System

3

Summary

3.95 The 2000 British Crime Survey (BCS) indicates that victimisation rates are now at their lowest level since 1993. But when a crime is committed, victims want the CJS to deliver justice, protection and service. Victims and witnesses also want to put the crime behind them and get on with the rest of their lives.

3.96 The support for victims in the UK is already high by international standards and we have the most generous Criminal Injuries Compensation Scheme (CICS) in the world.[120] But the Government is determined to do still more to deliver a better deal for victims and witnesses – including the large number of victims whose crime is never solved and who do not have the satisfaction of seeing an offender brought to justice.[121]

To win the confidence of victims, they must be better served

3.97 The Government wants a greater proportion of those who commit crime to be brought to justice – but this will not happen unless victims and witnesses are willing to report crimes and where necessary go to court to give evidence. The public must have confidence that the criminal justice process will treat victims and witnesses well.

3.98 Despite witnesses' misgivings about the ability of the CJS to meet the needs of victims, the great majority (76 per cent) are satisfied with their treatment by the individual agencies of the CJS. But nearly 40 per cent of all witnesses, rising to 47 per cent for those who were victims, would not be happy to be a witness again. The ordeal of cross-examination is unpleasant for many, and other issues, such as lack of information, waiting to give evidence and feelings of intimidation, can also mar the experience.[122]

3.99 The Government has set targets to improve victim and witness satisfaction, measured by the annual BCS and a new witness survey. At the heart of our plans is a new and expanded *draft Victim's Charter*,[123] which has been produced in partnership with victims' groups, the courts, the police and the CPS.

We must build on our achievements

3.100 The Government has provided 50 per cent extra funding for Victim Support over the last four years to improve the service it gives to over one million victims and more than 100,000 witnesses each year. Victim Support has established the first national *victims' helpline*, which receives more than 1,000 calls a month and is rolling out a new *Witness Service* in magistrates' courts to ensure that worried witnesses have someone to help them when they attend court.

3.101 The Government has changed the law to protect vulnerable or intimidated witnesses and children.[124] For example, the victims of sex attacks may no longer be cross-examined in person in court by their alleged attacker or subject to unnecessary cross-examination about their previous sexual history. Vulnerable or intimidated witnesses will be helped to give their best evidence in court, through more support before the trial, help with any communication difficulties and, where necessary, giving evidence by live TV link or using video-recorded statements.[125]

---

[120]*Criminal Victimisation in Seventeen Industrialised Countries: Key Findings for the 2000 International Crime Victims Survey* (2001).

[121]Research has suggested that only three per cent of offences resulted in a criminal conviction or a police caution, and is based on the number of offences measured by the BCS compared with the number of convictions/cautions measured in official statistics. *Digest 4: Information on the Criminal Justice System in England and Wales* (1999).

[122]*Key Findings from the Witness Satisfaction Survey 2000* (forthcoming).

[123]Consultation on revised victim's charter published February 2001.

[124]Youth Justice and Criminal Evidence Act 1999.

[125]These measures were among 78 recommendations to help vulnerable or intimidated witnesses made in the 'Speaking Up for Justice' Report. All recommendations have been accepted and are in the process of being implemented. Report of the Interdepartmental Working Group on the treatment of Vulnerable or Intimidated Witnesses in the Criminal Justice System. Home Office, (1998).

3.102 The families of homicide victims deserve particular support and sensitivity. Family liaison police officers provide support and information to bereaved families, in co-operation with Victim Support, as well as gathering information and potential evidence. Following the Stephen Lawrence Inquiry, family liaison officers now work to agreed national guidelines and the Association of Chief Police Officers (ACPO) has established a national curriculum for their training.[126]

3.103 By reducing delays – particularly in the youth justice system – we are also helping victims. Swift justice means memories will not have faded, it reduces the potential for intimidation and allows victims to get on with their lives more quickly once the case is over.

'Alicia's' story[127]

Alicia is a 32 year old single parent with three children. She was assaulted by her partner.

After reporting the assault to the police, Alicia felt the officers who dealt with her case were *'very good, very understanding'*. She was told what would happen if she was called as a witness and told not to be frightened. The police gave her the telephone number of Victim Support whom she contacted.

Alicia was unhappy that the case took a year to come to trial. She wanted to put the assault behind her. She also felt that her evidence would be *'fresher'* in her mind.

Before the trial the Witness Service contacted her, and offered a familiarisation visit which she declined. She had been on jury service and had read a helpful leaflet explaining the roles of the court staff. Nevertheless she still felt *'very uncomfortable'* about acting as a witness.

Unfortunately, this court did not have separate waiting facilities for prosecution witnesses, so when Alicia arrived at court she found that she had to sit in the same area as the defendant. However, a Witness Service volunteer offered to sit with her; the police officer who dealt with her case accompanied her; and the Witness Service volunteer spoke to her before they entered the court together.

Alicia found the court room more modern and less formal than she expected, but was uncomfortable being so near the defendant. The prosecuting barrister sat with her before entering court, explained court procedures and answered her questions at the end. *'I expected [the defence cross-examination] to be ten times worse'* she said, but still found the experience upsetting.

The magistrates too had made her feel comfortable.

Overall Alicia was satisfied with the CJS, and would act as a witness again. *'People have to get what they deserve'*, she said.

---

[126]Recommendations 23 – 38, *The Stephen Lawrence Inquiry* (1999).

[127]Case study taken from an interview reported in *'Monitoring the satisfaction of witnesses with their treatment by the CJS: Additional Qualitative Interviews'*, Unpublished interim findings prepared for the Strategic Planning Group, January 2001.

Modernising the Criminal Justice System

Providing a better service for victims with a new Charter of Rights ...

3.104 We are revising the Victim's Charter and consulting with the aim of establishing statutory rights and a Victims' Ombudsman to champion victims' interests.[128]

> ### The new Victim's Charter proposes the following rights for victims:
>
> - **to be treated with dignity and respect;**
> - **to support;**
> - **to protection;**
> - **to give and receive information;**
> - **to compensation or reparation;**
> - **to a transparent criminal justice process.**

3.105 A new Victims' Ombudsman would have the power to investigate individual complaints and would act as a champion of victims' interests, working with the Government and the CJS to introduce changes to services which will benefit victims. Once consultation on the new Charter is complete, implementation will follow as soon as practicable.

3.106 We will use the new Victim's Charter to encourage better service. For example, the CPS and the Witness Service might arrange for familiarisation visits to courts in advance of trials and could welcome victims and witnesses at court on the day of the trial and put them at ease.

... by improving the effectiveness of witnesses' attendance at court ...

3.107 One of the frustrations for victims and witnesses is coming to court and having to wait for long periods before their case is called and in some cases being sent home without giving evidence. CJS agencies are working together to find further ways of reducing waiting times for witnesses and doing away with unnecessary attendance.[129] From April 2001 the LCD and the CPS will begin a six month pilot scheme to identify the reasons for ineffective trials, a principal cause of unnecessary witness attendance.

3.108 The Court Service is also extending the practice of providing booked trial dates in the Crown Court. Especially in longer trials that involve a large number of witnesses, everyone will benefit from the certainty of a fixed date.

... by keeping victims informed ...

3.109 Victims and witnesses want to be kept informed. Current performance is not good enough. Recent research has shown that over half of prosecution witnesses were not kept informed by the police about the progress of the case and over one third of all witnesses waited over three months after giving a statement before they heard anything about the case. Over 40 per cent were not told the verdict but had to find it out for themselves.[130]

3.110 From April 2001, the CPS will start to take over from the police the responsibility for keeping victims informed about the decisions for which the prosecution is responsible, implementing the recommendations of the Stephen Lawrence Inquiry Report and earlier Glidewell Review. The CPS will write to victims explaining key casework decisions, such as if charges are dropped or substantially altered. In particularly serious or sensitive cases victims will have the offer of a face-to-face meeting with the prosecutor. The service will be in place nationally by October 2002.[131]

---

[128]*A Review of the Victim's Charter* (forthcoming).

[129]The Trials Issues Group will analyse the relationship between waiting times and unnecessary attendance at magistrates' courts and the Crown Court to find ways of reducing both.

[130]*Key Findings from the Witness Satisfaction Survey 2000* (forthcoming).

[131]£3 million has been allocated in 2001-2 from the CJS reserve for the introduction by the CPS of this standard of service in 2001.

3.111 We are also improving arrangements for the victims of mentally disordered offenders. At present, where an offender is detained in a secure hospital under the Mental Health Act, victims are often not given information about their discharge from hospital or the conditions that apply because of concerns about medical confidentiality. The Government recognises the distress that this causes when victims are unable to obtain basic information such as when the offender is to be released. Reformed mental health legislation will meet these concerns, providing broader parity of treatment between the victims of mentally disordered offenders and other offenders.

... and by making services more convenient

3.112 We will use internet technology to give access to information at a time and place convenient to victims. Work is already in hand to develop systems for providing Crown Court case information, including results, online and will be piloted before the end of this year.

3.113 The UK Government portal – UKOnline – includes a 'Dealing with Crime' life episode, providing information on personal safety, reporting crime, dealing with crime, victim support and compensation. There are links to websites, like Victim Support and the Criminal Injuries Compensation Authority. During 2001 we aim to extend the UKOnline service to enable victims to report non-urgent minor crimes online.

Helping to deliver justice by giving victims a voice ...

3.114 From October 2001 we will be introducing victim personal statements. Victims (including bereaved relatives in homicide cases) will be able to give a statement in their own words to the police saying how the crime has affected their lives.[132] These statements may then be used throughout the

criminal justice process. For example, they might trigger the provision of support services or be used to register whether the victim wants to be kept informed of case progress.

3.115 In cases that proceed to arrest and charge, victim personal statements could be used by the CPS in bail applications; to inform decisions about the suitability of charge; to judge the strength and credibility of evidence; or to rebut false claims made by the defence in mitigation. Where a case is before the court, the statement could be used by the prosecutor at the point of sentence, for example to draw the court's attention to its powers to order compensation. The victim personal statement will also be made available to other criminal justice agencies after conviction. Thus the Parole Board might use a statement to inform its decision on parole.

3.116 From April 2001 the National Probation Service will have to consult the victims of violent and sexual offenders sentenced to at least 12 months in prison about what restrictions should be placed on the offender when released from custody. Victims of these offenders will also have the right to be informed by the Probation Service about the offender's release and any relevant conditions made.

... by ensuring victims are compensated ...

3.117 Wherever appropriate, sentencing should offer some recompense to victims. This issue is being examined through the current review of the sentencing framework. One option is for a framework which would require judges to consider including in every community sentence elements of punishment, rehabilitation and reparation to the victim.

---

[132] £4.6 million has been allocated in 2001-2 from the CJS Reserve for the introduction of victim personal statements in 2001.

3.118 Courts are already required to consider, in every case where there is a recognisable victim, whether the offender should be ordered to pay monetary compensation. The court collects the compensation, pays it to the victim and enforces the order if offenders default. However, too many offenders simply fail to pay up. This is not acceptable. The Government will consider how victims might be more swiftly compensated, including the possibility of a Victims Fund to ensure that every victim receives immediate payment of any compensation order. It would be for the courts to pursue defaulters.

3.119 Victims of violent crimes in Great Britain are entitled – whether an offender has been convicted or not – to compensation under the Criminal Injuries Compensation Scheme (CICS). Last year the Criminal Injuries Compensation Authority paid out £206 million to over 43,000 successful claimants.[133] This is more than all the other European schemes added together.

3.120 Following a consultation exercise,[134] the Government has just announced plans to improve the CICS. Subject to approval by Parliament and the Scottish Executive, the intention is to increase significantly the awards for victims of rape, sexual assault and child abuse, to increase the awards for victims of serious multiple injuries, to extend eligibility for fatal awards to bereaved partners of the same sex, and to increase most tariff levels by ten per cent.

… and by better protecting them against repeat victimisation

3.121 Recent analysis[135] has underlined just how significant is the problem of repeat victimisation. One in five victims of burglary in 1999 was a victim more than once in the year, with seven per cent being a victim three times or more. Over one in three victims of violent crimes was victimised again in the year and nearly one in five victimised three times or more. Repeat victimisation causes disproportionate suffering. It also means that by protecting victims, we can do a great deal to prevent future crime. The police have a key role in protecting against repeat victimisation.

The Huddersfield repeat victimisation project[136]

Huddersfield Police Division developed a strategy for reducing repeat victimisation, effectively moving from the *deflection* of offenders to their *detection*.

Responses to each crime were graded as 'bronze', 'silver' and 'gold'. All first time victims received 'bronze' level responses such as property marking and security upgrading. Repeat victims received more resource-intensive 'silver' and 'gold' measures, such as focused patrolling, and the use of vehicle tracking or silent intruder alarms.

The approach resulted in a reduction of 24 per cent in domestic burglary while arrests resulting from the installation of alarms increased from four per cent to 14 per cent. A local police officer said, "We like it because it's simple to do, it's fair to victims and we know what we promise will be delivered."

---

[133] *Home Office Annual Report 1999/2000* (2000).

[134] *Compensation for victims of violent crime: possible changes to the Criminal Injuries Compensation Scheme* (1999).

[135] Table A2.9, *The 2000 British Crime Survey* (2000).

[136] *Preventing Repeat Victimisation: the police officer's guide* (1997).

Increasing protection against witness intimidation

3.122 The intimidation of victims and witnesses is of continuing and growing concern.[137] Perpetrated across a wide range of crimes including domestic violence, sexual offences, racial and homophobic crimes and repeat victimisation, the true extent is difficult to assess. It is in the nature of the crime that those who suffer from intimidation will often be too afraid to acknowledge it. Intimidation can be perpetrated by anyone, no matter what their background, social or professional standing, and can take place at any time before, during and after the criminal justice process. In particular, it can affect those whose evidence is important to prosecutions. Intimidation can also deter eyewitnesses from reporting a crime to the police in the first place.

3.123 'Speaking Up for Justice'[138] published in June 1998, describes the key measures to be taken by the criminal justice agencies to enable vulnerable and intimidated witnesses to give their best evidence. For their part, the police are taking a number of steps to improve their response to and handling of an intimidated witness, including training officers, developing inter-agency protocols and actively participating in community schemes. Responsibility for deciding whether a witness is at risk lies with the police and depending upon their risk assessment, the witness and/or his family will be offered appropriate protection. These range from panic alarms in the home for low-level harassment to complete relocation, sometimes with a change of identity, in the most serious cases.

3.124 At court, we are improving facilities to ensure that prosecution witnesses are not forced to sit alongside potentially intimidating defendants and their families. Wherever separate waiting facilities cannot be provided we will offer mobile phones or pagers to witnesses to enable them to wait where they feel comfortable and be called back when they are needed. New measures will also be introduced to help witnesses give evidence in court.

3.125 Witness intimidation in criminal proceedings is an offence and is covered by section 51 of the Criminal Justice and Public Order Act 1994. We aim to provide the same protection for witnesses in civil cases. This will mean better protection for witnesses giving evidence in proceedings for breaches of community sentences or proceedings to grant anti-social behaviour orders.[139]

Helping victims to move on after crime

3.126 Victims need to move on from the crime they have suffered and may want help to do so from agencies outside the CJS. Those who work in the CJS should ensure that victims receive appropriate referrals to agencies such as Victim Support, Rape Crisis, Shelter, and Citizen's Advice Bureau to help with a range of practical problems, such as home security insurance, dealing with housing authorities, employers, schools or social services.

3.127 The Government is also encouraging action by outside bodies to mitigate the effects of crime, for instance, through the use of insurance with rent schemes (see box).

---

[137]For example, eight per cent percent of all criminal victimisation incidents measured in 1998 led to some form of intimidation, mostly in the form of verbal abuse. About half of those intimidated felt the offender's motive was to 'annoy' or 'upset' them. Eight per cent thought it was to prevent them from giving evidence to the police or at court. *Victim and Witness Intimidation: Findings from the British Crime Survey* (2000).

[138]*Speaking Up for Justice, Report of the Interdepartmental Working Group on the Treatment of Vulnerable or Intimidated Witnesses in the Criminal Justice System* Home Office (June 1998).

[139]Criminal Justice and Police Bill (2001).

Modernising the Criminal Justice System

Insurance with rent schemes

Recent research has shown that up to a fifth of households have no home contents insurance. Often, people living in high crime neighbourhoods with high premiums are least able to afford insurance. So those who are more likely to be victims of crime lose out.[140]

Through insurance with rent schemes, the local authority or social housing landlord arranges group insurance policies and deals with the collection of premiums. Tenants get insurance they might not otherwise be able to afford and insurers benefit by having one large transaction instead of many small policies. These schemes already cover 1.7 million households nationally. The Government wants to see that extended.

The Housing Corporation is working with the National Housing Federation and the Association of British Insurers to examine the best way for these schemes to operate. They expect to publish guidance on best practice in March 2001.

Putting things right when mistakes are made

3.128 Like any other human system, the criminal justice process sometimes makes mistakes. In very rare cases these will have tragic consequences for individuals and their families. When mistakes are made, the victims of those errors want an apology and they want action. If there has been negligence, they want someone to be held accountable. The Criminal Cases Review Commission investigates suspected miscarriages of justice and criminal justice agencies already have procedures for dealing with complaints. Those with grievances may also have a route to the Parliamentary Ombudsman.

3.129 However the Government is committed to improving the situation. So for example, we intend to replace the existing Police Complaints Authority with a new Independent Police Complaints Commission.[141] This new system will be more accessible and open, and will allow independent investigations of more serious complaints. The Victims' Ombudsman would also investigate complaints and champion victims' interests.

---

[140]The 1998 BCS showed that 18 per cent of households nationally did not have home contents insurance. Economically disadvantaged homes were the least likely to have insurance: around a half (49 per cent) of those living in accommodation rented from a council or housing association were not insured and almost a half (47 per cent) of these said it was at least in part due to the expense. The 1998 BCS also shows that those least likely to have insurance are more at risk of burglary. 8.6 per cent of uninsured households experienced a burglary in 1997 while five per cent of insured households were burgled. *Burglary of Domestic Dwellings: Findings from the British Crime Survey* (1999).

[141]Details of the Government's proposal are set out in *Complaints Against the Police: Framework for a New System* (2000).

The police

Key measures

Delivering sustained reductions in crime and increasing public reassurance by:

- A 21 per cent cash increase in police funding over the period 2000-01 to 2003-04, including £500 million to fund Airwave – a new national secure digital radio system.

- An additional 9,000 recruits over and above what forces would otherwise have recruited over the period 2000-01 to 2002-03, which should take overall police numbers to their highest ever level by March 2003.

- An increase in trained detective capability including, where necessary, opportunities to recruit people with relevant specialist skills from other fields.

- An expansion of the DNA database to cover the whole active criminal population by April 2004.

- A new joint central body to oversee the development and specification of new technology and ICT with all forces required to take up the resulting systems.

- Every force expected to report to the local community on a ward-by-ward basis on what it will do to increase police visibility and accessibility.

- An on-going commitment to complete the implementation of the Stephen Lawrence Inquiry Report, including a new Independent Police Complaints Commission.

- Experimental accreditation of security or patrol staff from other organisations, working under police co-ordination to deliver improved community safety.

- Ensuring that police recruitment and retention reflect modern employment needs, allowing varied working patterns and entry and exit at different points in an individual's career.

- Improving leadership and training at all levels, including a new Leadership Development Board to support the senior appointments process.

- Major changes to the shape of police training, including a new National Training Organisation to set occupational standards for key ranks and a new core curriculum to deliver those standards.

- Best Value targets for crime reduction shared by the police and local authorities from April 2001.

Police performance is crucial to the performance of the Criminal Justice System as a whole ...

3.130 The police have a pivotal role in the CJS. The actions of the courts, prisons and Probation Service can only be triggered once the police have identified a suspect and gathered evidence sufficient to warrant a prosecution. However, a great deal of police time and effort is not devoted to the courts. Instead it involves reducing or preventing crime, particularly in statutory partnerships with local authorities and others under the Crime and Disorder Act 1998. In addition the police have a key task in maintaining a sense of public reassurance and confidence in a safe society.

3.131 Balancing these competing demands poses real problems. There is no automatic correlation between crime rates and the public's feelings of reassurance, and the most reassuring police activity – uniformed foot-patrol – is (by itself) not the most effective way of reducing or detecting crime.

… but the police face challenges as never before

3.132 At the same time, the social and technological context is changing rapidly. During the second half of the last century, respect for authority diminished. The internet and the mobile phone have not only provided new tools for criminals, and new targets for criminal activity, but also new means of seeking police assistance. Large scale smuggling of tobacco and alcohol has increased significantly. Organised crime – long involved in the drug trade – has now moved into people trafficking as well.

3.133 The courage and dedication of individual officers can only go so far in responding to these pressures. But as with all other institutions – private and public sector – how police officers are organised, managed and led can make a huge difference to their effectiveness at any given level of resources. The Government has been working with the police service to identify the priorities for police action and to provide the means to deliver them. This section sets out recent measures and new developments aimed at providing the most effective means of meeting the twin aims of reducing crime and increasing public reassurance.

Helping the police to reduce crime

3.134 The Government has recently taken a number of major steps to support the police in reducing crime, building on those in the 1998 Comprehensive Spending Review:

- Spending Review 2000 has increased funds for policing from £7.7 billion in 2000-01 to £9.3 billion in 2003-04, a rise of over 21 per cent.

- This includes £500 million to fund Airwave – a new secure digital radio system allowing radio communication across force boundaries and the supply of data direct to officers on the beat.

- An additional 9,000 recruits are being centrally funded, over and above the number forces would otherwise have recruited over the period 2000-01 to 2002-03. Assuming forces' current projections for wastage and recruitment hold good, police numbers should reach 128,000 by March 2002, and record numbers by March 2003. The number of civilian staff has already increased by 1,000 since March 1997 and stands at record levels of 54,000.

- The DNA database is being expanded to include the profiles of the whole of the active criminal population by April 2004.

- Under the Best Value regime, police authorities have set targets for the reduction of domestic burglary, vehicle crime and, in five major cities, robbery. By April 2005 these are intended to deliver an overall reduction of 25 per cent in recorded burglary, 30 per cent in vehicle crime (by April 2004), and 14 per cent in robbery in major cities.

- The Crime and Disorder Act 1998 created a statutory duty for local authorities and the police, in partnership with other agencies, to devise and implement local crime and disorder reduction strategies; it also required all local authorities and police authorities to do all that they reasonably can in carrying out their various functions to prevent crime and disorder.

3.135 The Audit Commission notes that 'There remain … significant variations in performance between police forces. These variations cannot simply be explained by differences in workload or by the varying circumstances forces face.'[142]

3.136 It is to enable the whole service to meet the foreseeable challenges as effectively as possible, that the Government has been in discussion with the leaders of the police service[143] to determine how best to modernise the service to meet the twin challenges of reducing crime and delivering public reassurance.

3.137 Tackling crime is a core function of the police. This is more than responding to individual incidents, but involves engaging with criminality in all forms and at every stage. The use of analysis, intelligence and investigative skills are essential to direct police activity into preventing crime and to gathering the evidence to secure convictions. But the quality and availability of crime specialists is only one aspect of tackling criminality. To achieve the best outcomes requires the coordination of standards and technical support across the service, as well as links to other law enforcement agencies operating at the national level. Building up all these approaches is essential to reverse the historical decline in clear up rates.

… through the best possible use of skilled personnel …

3.138 A highly trained specialist detective capability is critical to success. But it is becoming increasingly difficult to find enough experienced detectives and the pressures in some forces are such as to deter applications:

'Her Majesty's Inspector [of Constabulary] is concerned that the relatively low application rate within the Metropolitan Police Service and nationally for senior detective posts will eventually lead to a dilution in the skills base of officers to the detriment of investigations. In one area of the [Metropolitan Police Service] seven vacancies at detective inspector level were advertised and resulted in only one applicant'.[144]

3.139 Over-specialisation can result in an elite 'force within a force' leading to a closed culture with risks of ethical failings or even corruption; but the other extreme, of constant rotation of officers between widely different functions, fails to make best use of individual skills and aptitudes, and works against the optimum delivery of any specialist function. An approach which allows a career anchor in a specialism, and some experience in other areas, may offer the best solution, along with the increasingly sophisticated strategies now being put in place to ensure higher levels of integrity whatever function is being undertaken.

3.140 Where there are gaps which cannot be filled by experience or potential within the service, then there should be opportunities to recruit people with relevant specialist skills in other fields whether from the private or public sector. The nature of such appointments should offer rewards and career paths to attract applicants of the required calibre.

3.141 Raising detection rates and ensuring the highest professional standards of investigation and evidence presentation will significantly increase the chances of offenders being brought to justice. Our aim is to ensure that skilled detective expertise is built up again, maintained with specialist training, and underpinned by effective management strategies to ensure proper supervision and the prevention of corruption.

---

[142]*Local Authority Performance Indicators 1998-99* (2000).
[143]ACPO, Association of Police Authorities, Police Superintendents' Association, Metropolitan Police, HM Inspectorate of Constabulary; the Police Federation attended the first meeting only.
[144]Paragraph 15.14, *Policing London 'Winning Consent'* (2000).

Modernising the Criminal Justice System

... through the use of methods that have been proved to work ...

3.142 A National Intelligence Model has been approved by ACPO, representing the best practice in tackling crime. At present it is in use in some forces but not others. All forces should be required to adopt a consistent approach following accredited best practice models. This should be an issue for police authorities in carrying out functional reviews under Best Value and for HM Inspectorate of Constabulary (HMIC).

3.143 In this and in other areas of accredited best practice, such as the publication of HMIC thematic inspections, the Best Value process may lead to implementation of recommendations nationally. But this could be a slow process and there is a case for considering giving the Home Secretary a power to require police forces to follow specified accredited practices, in the same way that he has a power to require police forces to make use of specified central services or facilities.[145]

... by having the best technical and scientific support ...

3.144 There is no current means of defining and delivering the best developments in technical and scientific support that commands the full confidence of the policing world. The police service may identify specific requirements that need to be operated on the same basis across the country, but – even when wholly funded by central Government – individual forces may still decline to participate. The Airwave project is a case in point. It cannot be in the public interest for national operational benefits to be jeopardised in this way.

3.145 Working with policing partners, we will establish a new joint central body to determine the requirements in technical, scientific and ICT developments, and to oversee product development. All forces would then be required to take up the resulting systems. Successful implementation of the results will depend on the capacity of any new systems to make use of data already stored on older 'legacy' systems and to establish links between different information sources. The speed with which the operational benefits would be gained will depend on the pace of migration from existing systems and the availability of any additional funding to support a faster roll-out.

... and by ensuring agencies co-operate effectively

3.146 Crime knows no administrative boundaries. Police working methods must be designed so that they too are not hindered by geographical or agency boundaries. With the growth of organised crime, the National Crime Squad cannot deal with every instance, but will need to be supplemented by force-level responses drawing on the same intelligence products from the National Criminal Intelligence Service (NCIS). Responding to national and international organised crime requires a consistent approach across police forces and between agencies. Organised crime, like any other organised business, involves strategic direction, operational and supply chains, and direct sales to customers. Drug trafficking is a classic example of how tackling the operation as a whole benefits both National Crime Squad objectives and those of the local force, as the criminally supplied addict will in turn engage in property crime to support his addiction.

---

[145]Section 57, Police Act 1996.

Supporting the police in their role of providing public reassurance …

3.147 There is no automatic correlation between levels of actual or recorded crime and the degree of public reassurance evident at any time. Nor is there any unambiguous way of measuring it. The BCS distinguishes between worry about victimisation and the effect of that concern on daily life; Audit Commission performance indicators give levels of public satisfaction with particular police functions;[146] and the 1999-2000 Survey of English Housing reports on the number of households that perceive crime to be a problem in their area.[147]

3.148 The level of public reassurance will reflect a range of factors, including the way a survey question is posed, personal experience, media reporting of crime figures, high profile reports of individual crimes, visibility and accessibility of the police, presence of uniformed staff on railway stations, security guards in shopping centres and many other factors.

3.149 Accurate recording and reporting of crime is important to ensure that the public gets a realistic view of crime levels. The Home Office and ACPO are working to improve the collection and reliability of recorded crime statistics so that they more closely reflect the actual experience of crime. We intend to publish BCS and recorded crime at the same time to provide a fuller and more sophisticated understanding of crime. Locally, forces need to work to build up a good understanding by the local media of what they are doing and why.

3.150 The service can and should do more to increase public reassurance by the visibility of uniformed officers, by making access to the police easier, and by ensuring that other sectors which can contribute to feelings of public safety do so in a way which is properly coordinated with police activity (see below).

3.151 Tackling these issues will require a strategy that reflects their importance and is backed up by a performance management regime that measures and drives activity. HMIC is currently undertaking a thematic inspection on visibility and accessibility. The Government does not believe that there is a single prescriptive formula that could be applied to all forces, but will be looking for a menu of options from which police management can select what will best meet local needs. These will be set out in a Toolkit and evaluated to develop best practice. Forces will be expected to report to the local community on the action being taken in their area on a ward by ward basis. Immediately apparent options are set out below.

… through greater visibility …

3.152 A visible police presence has immense value for reassurance. But there is no 'right' number of officers – in 1945 there were over 60,000 officers, today there are over 124,000 and rising towards an expected all time high of over 128,000. The immediate issue is to ensure that existing resources are being effectively managed. The approaches listed below are adopted in some areas but not others:

- Uniformed foot patrol is a key public expectation. But undirected foot-patrol will do little to reduce crime and will not increase public reassurance unless properly deployed to achieve this.[148] Intelligence-led patrolling, however, puts the officers where crime is more likely to occur and acts as a deterrent, as well as a reassurance. The deployment of officers for brief periods outside schools as their day ends, commuter stations in the rush hour, or other places used by large numbers of people at peak periods will have a considerable effect.

---

[146]Public satisfaction with foot patrols stands at 20 per cent (down from 23 per cent in 1998-99), with mobile patrols 43 per cent (down from 47 per cent), with 999 calls 82 per cent (down from 85 per cent), and for victims of domestic burglary 90 per cent (down from 91 per cent). *Local Authority Performance Indicators 98-99: Police and Fire Services* (2000).

[147]This has declined from 69 per cent in 1997-98 to 56 per cent in 1999-2000. *Housing Statistics Summary Number 7 (2000).*

[148]*Crime and police effectiveness* (1984).

- Doubling up officers on foot patrol or mobile patrol may be necessary for operational or safety reasons, but it should not be the norm. Assaults on police officers have in fact decreased by 25 per cent over the period 1993-94 to 1999-00.[149] In many areas, particularly in daylight, a proper risk assessment could not justify double patrolling. Patrolling singly not only doubles the area covered, but the officer patrolling singly is more likely to engage with local people than if patrolling in company with another.

- Use of civilian support staff, both in custody suites and in case preparation units, can enable officers to return to patrol duty after making an arrest far more quickly than would otherwise be the case.

- There are operational reasons that require officers to wear plain clothes, but in other circumstances officers could normally be expected to wear uniform.

- Government action in reducing paperwork requirements will also help increase effective officer time. As a result of a recent report[150] revised guidance has been issued to the police reducing by over a third the number of forms to be completed in passing cases to the CPS. One of the aims of the current review of the Police and Criminal Evidence Act 1984 codes of practice is to take every opportunity to reduce the administrative burdens on the police. In addition we are investing in an ICT based custody and case preparation system that will remove the need for duplication of information on different forms and between different agencies.

... through greater accessibility of police services ...

3.153 The public's relations with the police will be significantly affected by the ease with which it is possible to report a crime or raise concerns. If the police station is some distance away, the counter is busy with a queue, or a non-emergency call takes too long to be answered, then confidence fall. Options for reducing these problems include:

- use of mobile police stations;

- 'virtual' police stations in shopping centres, with an ICT link providing access to information and allowing reporting of minor crimes, progress enquiries and information;

- providing 'surgery' access to ward officers at one stop shops with other public services;

- maintaining a part time police presence in public buildings in rural areas, involving regulars, part-time officers, specials or civilian volunteers;[151] and

- arrangements to contact the police for crime reporting or other purposes by internet.

Police office in a church

The vestry of Holy Trinity Church, in the South Yorkshire village of Wentworth, now also serves as a local police office. PC Anne Hirst, who covers Wentworth and Harley, plans to hold a weekly 'surgery' there for the local community.

---

[149]*HMIC Annual Force Statistical Returns* (various years).
[150]*Making a difference – reducing police paperwork* (2000).
[151]The options for rural sub-post offices will be considered by an inter-departmental group that is being formed to consider the role of post offices as 'general Government practitioners' and internet access points.

… and by promoting effective partnership

3.154 Policing by consent is a fundamental and valued principle of British arrangements. But the principle of consent cannot mean that the community delegates the whole of its concern for its own safety to a professional body. Individual and collective responsibilities remain and should find proper expression alongside the powers and functions that can only properly be exercised by a trained and accountable professional police force.

3.155 The principle is equally apparent in other sectors. Health care is provided through doctors, nurses, paramedics, ambulance crews, pharmacists, St John's Ambulance, trained first aiders, self medication, but is directly affected by individuals' lifestyle choices about exercise, smoking and drinking.

3.156 The Crime and Disorder Act 1998 established a duty for local authorities, the police, and bodies working in partnership with them, to produce strategies for the reduction of crime and disorder in the local area. Partnership activity is aimed at reducing rather than detecting crime, but the engagement of different agencies can have a significant effect on levels of public reassurance as well.

3.157 There has always been a wide range of people contributing to community safety in various forms. These include park keepers (some with constabulary powers), security guards in shopping centres, car park attendants, neighbourhood wardens, night club bouncers and the private security industry. The issue for policing is how these various activities can be co-ordinated to make the most effective contribution to making safer communities.

Neighbourhood Wardens

Neighbourhoods Wardens promote community safety, working in and with communities to reduce the fear of crime, strengthen community spirit, and report issues to the police, Local Authority and Housing Associations. Across the country and abroad, similar schemes have had a noticeable effect in disadvantaged neighbourhoods. Wardens complement the work of the police, responding to antisocial behaviour, racial harassment and promoting community safety.

DETR and the Home Office have jointly allocated £18.5 million until 2003-4. A total of 86 schemes across England and Wales have been awarded funding from the Neighbourhood Warden programme.

3.158 The private security industry will be subject to regulation under the Private Security Bill now before Parliament. But no attempts have been made to link the overall contribution to public safety made by different bodies in a local area. The Government believes that there is scope for some evaluated schemes to determine the effect on public reassurance of the police accrediting and coordinating a range of independent bodies to work in conjunction with them in delivering community safety.

3.159 This might best be organised as a crime and disorder partnership initiative. Staff working on such schemes would be deployed to meet particular requirements and would not be diverted to meet other organisational priorities. They would not generally have the power of the constable and would be accountable to their employers, but their recognition as contributors to public safety would depend on police approval of the scheme in question. Their activities could be coordinated with policing needs by an officer with an enhanced role as community beat manager.

Supporting the police in giving reassurance to minority ethnic communities

3.160 Public reassurance must extend equally across all communities. Recent research findings from the BCS show a worrying gap in how different groups had been affected by police officers' behaviour in the previous five years:

'Twice as many black respondents (38 per cent) as white respondents (19 per cent) felt really annoyed. Asian respondents were also more likely than whites to have been annoyed by police behaviour (23 per cent). Generally the reasons given were that the police had been rude or unfriendly (39 per cent), had behaved unreasonably (31 per cent) or had failed to do anything (26 per cent).'[152]

3.161 The Home Secretary has taken personal responsibility for oversight of the implementation of the Government's action plan in response to the Stephen Lawrence Inquiry Report's recommendations.

3.162 Over 70 per cent of the Report recommendations have now been implemented. Substantial progress has been made on the remaining recommendations. Key achievements so far include:

- a new ministerial priority for the police service to increase trust and confidence in policing amongst minority ethnic communities;

- a new code of practice on the reporting and recording of racist incidents, to be used by all relevant agencies to ensure a consistent and comprehensive approach;

- a new Action Guide to identifying and combating hate crime was launched by ACPO in September 2000 after extensive community consultation;[153] and

- the Race Relations (Amendment) Act 2000 outlaws race discrimination in law enforcement and other public functions not previously covered by the Race Relations Act 1976. It imposes a duty on public authorities to work towards the elimination of unlawful race discrimination and to promote equality of opportunity between persons of different racial groups.

3.163 Two of the recommendations of the Stephen Lawrence Inquiry Report refer directly to the police complaints system. The Government has set out its intentions in the proposals for reform of the system, including the replacement of the Police Complaints Authority by a new body, the Independent Police Complaints Commission.[154]

---

[152]*Policing and the public: findings from the 2000 British Crime Survey* (2001).
[153]*Breaking the power of fear and hate* (2000).
[154]*Complaints Against the Police: Framework for a New System* (2000).

Provision for this reform will be made at the earliest legislative opportunity and, realistically, the new system would come into effect in April 2003 at the earliest.

3.164 The HMIC thematic inspection of the police service approach to race and community relations – the last of a trilogy of such inspections in the past five years – reported substantial progress across the vast majority of forces. The inspection noted evidence from minority ethnic communities of 'a renewal or, in some cases, a birth of confidence in their police'.[155] HMIC will support, encourage and monitor the service in consolidating and developing improvements.

Addressing police organisational issues ...

3.165 The present structure of 43 police forces across England and Wales reflects the historical development of the service. The Government has no present plans to amalgamate smaller forces with their neighbours, nor to move to a regional policing structure. While there are arguments for economies of scale from amalgamations, the Government is concerned that the administrative effort and operational disruption would interrupt present activity on crime reduction. The Government however remains open to respond positively to representations about boundaries, where increased effectiveness in reducing crime would justify the inevitable disruption, as it did in 1998 in respect of the Metropolitan Police Area.

3.166 Under Best Value, police authorities are required to consider the scope for collaboration and co-operation in reviewing all their functions. This may well lead to joint or regional handling of specific functions, achieving greater efficiency and effectiveness, without the disruption of institutional amalgamations.

3.167 HMIC will be examining the issues that determine the effectiveness of different sizes of police force. They will aim to set out factors which forces and police authorities should take into account in determining whether their business is best delivered through current arrangements, through collaboration with neighbours, or, if the benefits really outweigh the costs, through formal amalgamation.

... the role of the Basic Command Unit ...

3.168 Basic Command Units (BCUs) are the prime means by which local crime reduction and public reassurance are delivered. However, they cannot be wholly autonomous and depend on specialist support from Force Headquarters, in both operational and administrative matters, and may need support from other BCUs to deal with major incidents. Some major incidents and specialist activities can only be handled at a Headquarters level.

3.169 BCUs must function as an integral part of a wider policing operation across the force as a whole. But there is a need for greater clarity about the nature and extent of delegated authority that BCUs should exercise. The Audit Commission has been examining the relationships between BCUs and force headquarters. The Government will consider whether further steps are necessary in the light of their report.

3.170 Performance at BCU level varies considerably across the country. Recorded crime statistics now include performance in key crime categories by individual BCUs and by Crime and Disorder Reduction Partnerships, grouped in broadly similar categories. Work is in hand to group BCUs in similar families so that like can be compared with like. This should be available for the statistical bulletin to be published in July 2001.

---

[155]Executive Summary paragraph 24, *Winning the race – embracing diversity* (2001).

3.171 To recognise and encourage high performance, the Government has announced a BCU reward fund as part of the Spending Review 2000. Initially this will involve £5 million a year, to cover the costs both of BCU inspections by HMIC and a reward fund of some £4 million. Arrangements for determining the distribution of the fund are now being discussed with ACPO and the Association of Police Authorities (APA). The criteria are likely to reflect the success of a particular BCU in reducing crime and in raising public reassurance, in partnership with other local agencies.

... and personnel issues

(1) Constables

3.172 The core of policing depends on trained police officers carrying out functions requiring constabulary powers. At a time of full employment, the service must be seen as an attractive career option – to people from all backgrounds – and that there must be no artificial barriers which limit the pool of possible applicants. The service needs to recognise that contemporary employment patterns are moving away from the expectation of lifetime careers in a single organisation. Provision needs to be made for more flexible career management, recognising that it will be in the interests of the individual and of the organisation if people can join and leave the service at different stages in their careers. This may be essential to ensure that the service has within it the full range of skills to deliver functions ranging from community policing to tackling internet fraud.

3.173 The present arrangements for pay and conditions may not fully reflect the importance of several policing functions. The low application rates for Senior Investigating Officer posts have already been described. But equally importantly, there has been little to encourage officers in routine close contact with the community to regard that as a valued specialism. There are arguments for providing a capacity to progress as an experienced community officer without necessarily becoming a supervisor. A community beat officer could warrant additional rewards if the function included the coordination of the activities of contributors to public safety from other agencies. And there may be a case for pay differentials between officers working shifts and those working regular hours, or for arranging alternative shift patterns as has proved popular, for example, in Kent.

3.174 The requirements and expectations of both part-time officers and Special Constables need also to be considered. Under current regulations a part-time officer must work for at least 16 hours a week, preventing the community benefiting from a shorter period of duty which might nonetheless be of considerable value in rural areas. The contribution of Special Constables is also lower than it might be. A number now see the role as a means of trying out a police career before applying for regular service, helped by the Police Health and Safety Act 1997 which effectively requires the same standards of training and equipment for both Specials and Regulars. Overall, the number of Specials has been declining for some years and the Home Office is now exploring with ACPO and the APA ways of increasing the numbers recruited and retained as Specials.

3.175 A number of issues in the paragraphs above would of course require negotiation through existing statutory mechanisms.

(2) Civilians

3.176 The contribution of civilians, especially in bringing specialist skills to policing, will remain vital. The primary criterion for deciding whether a function should be handled by officers or civilians should be whether or not it requires the exercise of constabulary powers. Civilians are already making major contributions well beyond administrative and technical support: scenes of crime officers, crime pattern analysts and case preparation staff all make important contributions to crime reduction. The use of civilians in custody suite support roles can free up arresting officers to return to the street much faster than would otherwise be the case. And there is no reason in principle why civilians with a background in insurance fraud or ICT could not contribute directly to the detection of crime.

Civilian investigators in Wiltshire

Wiltshire Constabulary has advertised for civilian investigators to deal with minor offences such as shop-lifting. The scheme will be piloted in the Chippenham division and, if successful, it will be extended across the force.

3.177 To recruit the right calibre of civilian staff for specialist functions, suitable career patterns will need to be available.

(3) Ancillary functions

3.178 In recent years, many ancillary functions have been transferred from the police, either to local authorities or outsourced to the private sector. These functions have included traffic wardens, parking, and much traffic management, custody escort, court security, and from 1 April 2001, fine enforcement. The establishment of the CPS released a large number of police inspectors from work in magistrates' courts as prosecutors. We shall continue to examine whether further ancillary functions could be handled by other agencies.

(4) Leadership

3.179 Present arrangements for filling senior posts in the police service do not fully meet the needs of the service, the applicants, or the appointing police authority. A completely open market may result in the best candidate not being available for the most demanding position, and limits opportunities for the development of those with the potential to rise furthest.

3.180 Without derogating from the duty of police authorities to make appointments of ACPO rank officers, the Government intends to bring in a more structured approach. This will be centred on a new Leadership Development Board chaired by HM Chief Inspector of Constabulary. The Board will oversee the senior appointments process, the new accelerated promotion scheme, and the Extended Interview process – the gateway to senior ranks. The membership will include representatives of ACPO, APA, HMIC, Home Office, and the police staff associations.

3.181 A number of other needs must also be met to fit the service for the future:

- police authorities need to enhance their professionalism and capabilities, particularly in relation to personnel matters;

- joint training and secondments with other criminal justice agencies should become a routine part of senior officer development;

- at all levels in the service more attention needs to be paid to the requirement for leadership abilities; and

- partnership working calls for a different emphasis on leadership skills, requiring the ability to achieve outcomes through exercising influence and negotiation, outside a command structure.

3.182 These issues will need to be taken forward through formal training arrangements (*see paragraph below*) as well as the identification of good practice in the Toolkit on partnerships.

(5) Training

3.183 The Government is making major changes to the shape of police training, including measures in the Criminal Justice and Police Bill currently before Parliament:

- a new employer-led National Training Organisation (NTO) for the police;

- a new core curriculum to set out the training needed to deliver the occupational standards set by the NTO. Standards will be tested by qualifications for certain roles;

- a Central Police Training and Development Authority will be a focus for the development and promotion of professional excellence across the police service; and

- a new dedicated training inspectorate within HMIC, headed by a lay inspector, and new powers for the Home Secretary to ensure that high standards are met.

Continuing to build and support effective partnership issues

3.184 Reducing crime depends on far more than just the actions of the police. Individual choices, social conditions, opportunities and deterrents will all affect the level of crime in any area. The creation of statutory Crime and Disorder Reduction Partnerships at local level recognises the contribution that other agencies can make and the lead that partnerships should take locally. Consultation with communities in the light of the initial audits undertaken by the partnerships showed that in many areas the main public concerns were not only about major crime but also about nuisance issues that affected the quality of life and feelings of public reassurance. Partnerships are thus essential for the delivery of both crime reduction and public reassurance.

3.185 The same Best Value targets for crime reduction set by police authorities will apply from April 2001 to local authorities. This will create joint and several accountability for specific crime reduction targets, and can only be delivered in partnership.

3.186 The Home Office has helped the work of local partnerships by publishing 'Toolkits' on its crime reduction website.[156] Twenty-two are being published between January and March this year, covering topics ranging from Persistent Young Offenders to Using Intelligence and Information Sharing. The appointment by the Home Office of ten Crime Reduction Directors and their teams in each of the English regions and in Wales has provided further support, giving a focus for spreading best practice, engaging and supporting partnerships, and making the best use of available funding opportunities.

3.187 We now need to see local authorities, police authorities and others responding fully to the requirements of section 17 of the Crime and Disorder Act 1998, and taking the crime prevention implications into account in carrying out all their duties. As statutory members of Crime and Disorder Reduction Partnerships, local authorities should see the benefits for their own business and for their communities of implementing s.17, but ultimately this is a matter to be checked through Best Value reviews and inspections.

3.188 Crime reduction partnerships need to work closely with Neighbourhood Renewal initiatives. Reduction of crime is an integral part of the vision to improve dramatically the social conditions in the most deprived neighbourhoods, and community policing will be critical to building up local confidence that the problems of a particular neighbourhood can be turned round permanently. Local Strategic Partnerships will be responsible for driving forward work on neighbourhood renewal, agreeing and implementing community strategies reflecting local priorities for improving quality of life. They will also provide a framework for rationalising and improving the links between other local partnerships, to develop a more coherent, joined up approach and deliver better services to local people.

3.189 At national level linkages between policy, programmes and funding across Government departments will become increasingly important. The cross-departmental review of crime reduction in the Spending Review 2000 recorded a number of new initiatives[157] covering contributions to crime reduction from the DH, the DfEE, and the DETR. Policies and funding relating to alcohol, truancy or planning have a direct bearing on police activity, and, if properly co-ordinated, will simultaneously deliver better departmental outcomes and increased crime reduction.

Conclusion

3.190 The reform programme for policing set out in this section represents a major development of policing in England and Wales. Some elements of it are already well underway with legislation before Parliament; other parts will need considerable development work and discussion before the policy can be finalised; and some areas are clearly experimental and will have to be judged on the results of carefully evaluated trials. In setting the direction of travel the Government has drawn on the advice and guidance of the police service itself, police authorities and HMIC, to define the most pressing changes needed to deliver sustained reductions in crime and growing public reassurance.

---

[156]www.crimereduction.gov.uk/toolkits
[157]Chapter 28, www.hm-treasury.gov.uk/sr2000

Modernising the Criminal Justice System

International and organised crime

Key measures

- Developing an integrated intelligence capability, analysing information from local, national and international sources to inform strategic priorities and co-ordinate operational responses, underpinned by a National Intelligence Model in use by every police force in the UK.

- A pool of experts in investigating and prosecuting serious and organised criminals, working closely together on cases from an early stage. Inter-agency co-operation supported by increased secondments and joint training, delivered by a new National Specialist Law Enforcement Centre.

- New legal framework, such as a new single offence of fraud and consideration of a new offence to tackle organised criminal conspiracy.

- Mutual recognition of court decisions in the EU to speed up legal co-operation including freezing of assets, and a review of extradition to introduce new fast track measures for the handover of fugitives from justice.

- A National Hi-Tech Crime Strategy with £25 million funding for police forces and the creation of a new Hi-Tech Crime Unit based at the National Crime Squad.

- The UK at the heart of international co-ordination against organised crime, including implementation of agenda set out at the Tampere Special European Council.

- Proceeds of Crime Bill: new arrangements for recovery of criminal assets including of a new asset recovery agency, with more of the resulting receipts to be channelled into crime fighting and drugs prevention.

- New powers for the Financial Services Authority to tackle money laundering and exploitation of financial services by organised criminals, backed up by increased funding for the Economic Crime Unit at the National Criminal Intelligence Service (NCIS).

The serious threat from organised and international crime

3.191 Organised crime is perpetrated by well-organised, often international, gangs and networks, usually motivated by financial gain though some have other motivations like terrorism or child pornography. Their activities employ huge financial resources, generating profits worth billions of pounds. A relatively small number of organisations is responsible for a huge amount of crime committed.[158] The coherence and effectiveness of the UK's response has improved greatly in recent years. But organised crime will continue to evolve, and we must ensure we are equipped to stay one step ahead of the criminals.

---

[158]It has been estimated for example that 400 individuals hold criminal assets worth at least £440 million – *Recovering the Proceeds of Crime* (2000).

3.192 Current growth areas in organised crime include fraud, trafficking in drugs, people and tobacco smuggling.[159] Since most organised criminals are motivated by profit, they can and do switch between activities on the basis of dispassionate calculations of risk and reward. In recent years, criminal groups have exploited the growth in international trade, reduced border controls, the collapse of the former Soviet Union and Yugoslavia and new means of communication and money transmission.

Organised crime – some indicators

Range of activities

There were some 965 organised criminal groups known to be active in the UK in 1999. This chart gives an indication of their activities, as far as they are known to NCIS. Many groups are involved in more than one activity.

% of known groups involved in activity

Activities of organised criminals

Source: NCIS

Heroin and cocaine seizures

Heroin and cocaine seizures

No of seizures

■ Heroin ■ Cocaine

Source: Home Office

Note: Cocaine figures exclude crack

---

[159]Source: NCIS. See box for an indication of the range and impact of organised crime. Reliable figures are difficult to obtain, and those quoted are not intended to be comprehensive or fully representative.

Modernising the Criminal Justice System

3.193 Organised crime involves what are effectively large, diverse and multinational businesses. Their organisational structure can vary, from long established hierarchical groups specialising in particular types of criminality (eg drug trafficking), to loose conspiracies which come together for a particular purpose (eg to commit a fraud). They can employ complex corporate and financial structures, either to commit their crimes, or to launder the proceeds.

3.194 Whilst the reach of organised crime is global, its impact is local. Larger criminal enterprises often facilitate local crime, for example by providing expertise in handling stolen goods, or supplying local drug markets. Organised criminals create misery for communities and provide dangerous role models for those on the fringes of criminality.

3.195 Organised crime also generates unfair competition for legitimate companies – through 'front' businesses used to launder profits. It can threaten the integrity of financial markets and financial institutions, creating a risk for ordinary investors. And every one of us is affected – as a taxpayer – when tax and duties are evaded.

International crime – local impact

Organised criminals are responsible for much of the supply of drugs to the UK. It is estimated that about two thirds of persistent offenders have serious drug problems. Addicts of heroin and crack have average annual incomes from crime of £13,000, accounting for between a third and a fifth of all acquisitive crime.[160]

Organised crime – some more indicators

Seizures of smuggled tobacco

Year	1998/99	1999/2000	2000/01*
Numbers of cigarettes seized	560m	1.7bn	2.1bn

* Figures for 2000/01 are for the first 9 months only

Illegal migration

Of the following numbers, it is estimated that 75 per cent have had their entry facilitated by organised criminal groups.

	1990	1991	1992	1993	1994	1995	1996	1997	1998	1999[2]
Number of persons [1]	3,300	4,460	5,670	5,780	7,540	10,820	14,560	14,390	16,500	21,170

(1) Illegal entry detections by date notices of illegal entry issued. "Detected" relates to those persons identified by Local Enforcement Offices and treated as offenders. This will include a number of people who have already made themselves known to the Home Office through applications.

(2) Provisional. 2000 figures are not published until the autumn.

---

[160] *Drugs and crime: the results of the second developmental stage of the NEW-ADAM programme* (2000).

A solid foundation to counter this threat

3.196 Since 1997 the Government has been strengthening the strategic response to organised crime. There now exists for the first time a coordinated multi-agency strategy, based on an agreed assessment of key threats. The box shows our achievements so far. But there is more work to be done. Based on the new multi-agency strategy, the Government is now considering making available additional funding to support the fight against key organised crime threats over the next few years.

3.198 Each of these areas involves international initiatives. The UK is determined to show the leadership necessary to deliver international coordination, and to pursue every opportunity to prevent and fight international organised crime in international fora. We will use every lever available to influence other countries to take the threat as seriously as we do.

The fight against organised crime – recent milestones

- **Publication of first 10-year UK anti-drugs strategy and appointment of UK anti-drugs co-ordinator – 1998.**

- **National Criminal Intelligence Service (NCIS) established on a statutory basis – 1998.**

- **Creation of the National Crime Squad (see Annex F) – 1998.**

- **Creation of Scottish Drug Enforcement Agency (see Annex F) – 1998.**

- **First firm targets for reducing drugs availability – 1998.**

- **UK leads Tampere agenda on EU police and judicial cooperation – 1999.**

- **Regulation of Investigatory Powers Act – 2000.**

- **Financial Services and Markets Act provisions on money laundering – 2000.**

- **Publication of strategy for reducing tobacco smuggling – 2000.**

3.197 The key areas for further work are to ensure:

- better strategic intelligence;

- appropriate laws;

- well coordinated skills and technology; and

- an effective means of depriving criminals of their assets.

Developing better strategic intelligence

3.199 Since organised crime is complex and changing, our response to it must be based on detailed and up to date information which is shared effectively between law enforcement agencies. We have made progress in recent years. In partnership with operational agencies, NCIS develops, collates, disseminates and analyses criminal intelligence. A new unit within the Joint Intelligence Organisation in the Cabinet Office provides high level assessment of criminal intelligence. And increasingly, the security and intelligence agencies are applying their specialised skills against organised crime at home and abroad, contributing to intelligence assessment and operational support.

3.200 But we still need to understand more about organised criminal activities. Information from the most comprehensive range of sources, from satellite data to street level informants, must feed into systematic research and analysis to develop an integrated picture. This requires that intelligence be shared between all relevant agencies, using effective ICT links and agreed procedures and data handling standards.

3.201 The National Intelligence Model, developed by NCIS, provides a template for this information exchange. We shall provide over £10 million to help fund the implementation of the model at national and local level. It sets out how local law enforcement can feed into a regional, national and international analysis, and receive in return detailed pictures of local crime informed by that analysis. The model is already in place in several police forces, and is being adopted across the country. Within a few years, officers should be able to have mobile, online access to databases to allow them to report and obtain the intelligence they need, where and when they need it. The model will be supported by information exchange with EU partners, through Europol, and, when implemented, the Schengen Information System, which NCIS will receive £3.3 million to take forward.

3.202 Effective data sharing arrangements are little good if the relevant Government agencies lack the legal powers to use them, and the common data standards do not exist to permit information to be shared in a timely and user-friendly manner. The Government attaches high priority to protecting the rights of individuals, as its introduction of the Human Rights Act demonstrates. But an effective response to crime requires unnecessary barriers to information exchange between crime fighting agencies to be removed. The Criminal Justice and Police Bill, when enacted, will make it easier for the Inland Revenue and Customs & Excise to disclose information to other appropriate authorities for use in criminal proceedings.

Tackling identity fraud

Some criminals will deliberately misrepresent a person's identity, to gain a benefit or service to which they are not entitled. This ID fraud threatens financial institutions as well as the individual whose identity may be stolen.

The DSS Counter Fraud Investigation Branch has worked with the Inland Revenue, the Office for National Statistics, the Passport Agency and the Immigration Service to counter the hijacking of identities. A memorandum of understanding has also been signed with the police on sharing information.

This has led to more detection of false documents and closed legal loopholes, for instance, concerning the identities of deceased infants.

3.203 A strategic approach to tackling organised crime needs to be matched by effective, joined-up law enforcement and intelligence. It requires the coordinated effort of the range of agencies involved using their varied skills and experience to work together at local and international level. Within the Organised Crime Strategy Group chaired by the Home Office, there are different groups which bring together the key players ensure the development of effective policies, intelligence and operational action against organised crime threats (see box).

Orchestrating the response – tackling drug trafficking

The Concerted Inter-Agency Drugs Action group (CIDA), chaired by Customs & Excise, focuses the efforts of the key law enforcement and intelligence organisations on reducing the availability of heroin and cocaine in support of the Government's overall anti-drugs strategy. The Group ensures that up-to-date knowledge and intelligence on trafficking routes and methodologies, money laundering techniques and developing trends are turned into targeted action to tackle the problem.

In a joint operation in October last year involving the National Crime Squad and Customs & Excise, two vessels were intercepted off the Isle of Wight, nine people were arrested and cocaine with an estimated street value of £40 million was seized.

Environmental Crime

The extent of transnational environmental crime, covering the illegal trade in wildlife and endangered species, hazardous waste, ozone-depleting substances and radioactive substances, is difficult to assess but is a matter of increasing concern.

There is evidence that organised crime groups are becoming involved in the illegal trade in ozone depleters, with chlorofluorocarbons being transported from Russia and China to the United States via Europe. The international response has involved both G8 and Interpol.

The UK's Interpol Environmental Crime Group forms the core of a domestic inter-agency information sharing network. Its wildlife crime sub-group, the Partnership for Action against Wildlife Crime, is currently working establish a National Wildlife Crime Unit to collect and disseminate intelligence on the most serious wildlife crimes.

We will provide appropriate legal powers

3.204 The CJS needs adequate legal powers and appropriate procedures to deal with organised criminals and the technology they use. The Regulation of Investigatory Powers Act 2000 has already updated the law to take account of rapidly evolving technology. It ensures that intelligence and law enforcement agencies continue lawfully to intercept communications and conduct surveillance on serious criminals, within the bounds of the Human Rights Act. The recently published Criminal Justice and Police Bill will update powers of lawful seizure of evidence to take account of electronic data.

3.205 To strengthen the law, we are considering a prosecution right of appeal against adverse judicial decisions in certain circumstances. The Government also favours introducing a new single offence of fraud to increase the likelihood of successful fraud prosecutions.[161] We will also consider whether there is a need to introduce new offences to tackle organised criminal conspiracy. Corruption is an important aspect of organised crime, and we are proposing a new provision to give the UK jurisdiction over bribery offences committed by UK nationals overseas, and measures to help developing countries to prevent corruption.[162]

[161]The Law Commission is currently examining how such an offence could be defined.
[162]The proposals are made respectively in *Raising Standards and Upholding Integrity: the Prevention of Corruption (2000)* and *Eliminating World Poverty: Making Globalisation Work for the Poor* (2000.)

3.206 Court proceedings arising out of organised crime can be complex, and the issues of law reform and rules of evidence discussed above could be particularly relevant to them. We are also taking measures to ensure adequate protection of witnesses and victims, which can be particularly important in organised crime cases.

3.207 On the international front, a review of extradition to be published shortly will include recommendations for swifter and simpler procedures. Key proposals include legislation for fast track extradition with our EU partners. Discussions are already taking place with some of our closest partners to develop arrangements on a bilateral basis as forerunners to an EU instrument. We will also raise internationally the complex issue of what new arrangements may be needed to simplify the process for trying co-defendants from different jurisdictions.

We will provide coordinated skills and technology

3.208 As well as having appropriate powers and procedures, the CJS must also contain the specialist expertise needed to investigate and prosecute organised criminals effectively. It is already staffed by many highly skilled professionals. We must ensure they are given the training and technical support they need, and that their various specialist skills are well coordinated.

3.209 Staff interchange and secondment and joint training will foster closer working between key agencies and with our international partners. A new National Specialist Law Enforcement Centre will provide joint training in specialist investigative techniques for staff from NCIS, the National Crime Squad, the police and customs. We will also enhance the system for investigating fraud, with closer working between police services and the Serious Fraud Office, including through increased secondments. A multi-agency working group on improving the response to fraud is examining the options for more effective fraud investigation.

3.210 There is a need for a cadre of prosecutors expert in dealing in organised crime. Better links between investigation and prosecution would ensure that investigators fully understand the evidential requirements for successful prosecutions. So we will explore the potential for involving prosecutors earlier in the investigative process in serious cases. This may require new powers, for example to compel disclosure, and greater direct liaison by the CPS with their foreign counterparts. We must ensure effective links between the different prosecuting bodies, including the CPS, Customs & Excise and the Serious Fraud Office.

3.211 To enhance the technical resources available to law enforcement, the Government is establishing a National Technical Assistance Centre. This will provide a central facility to derive intelligible material from lawfully obtained encrypted computer data and computer-to-computer communications. We will pull strands into a comprehensive national strategy on e-crime to ensure that policy across the CJS takes account of the threats and opportunities provided by new technology. A new National Hi-Tech Crime Strategy, backed by £25 million of new funding, will increase our ability to tackle crime involving new technology. A new multi-agency Hi-Tech Crime Unit, hosted by the National Crime Squad, will begin operation in April 2001 to deal with the most serious and organised hi-tech offences, including those with transnational impact.

3.212 At the Special European Council at Tampere in 1999 the Prime Minister and his EU counterparts agreed a programme to improve EU police and judicial cooperation, based heavily on UK initiatives. The Tampere agenda includes:

- mutual recognition of court decisions in the EU to speed up judicial cooperation;

- the creation of a new judicial cooperation body, Eurojust, to improve the coordination of the investigation and prosecution of serious crime;

- joint investigative teams to combat cross-border crime;

- the foundation of a European Police College for joint training of senior law enforcement officers;

- developing the capability of Europol as an EU-wide agency to exchange and analyse criminal intelligence; and

- various initiatives for sharing best practice and facilitating common working, such as a European Crime Prevention Network and a European Police Chiefs Task Force.

3.213 The UK has been at the forefront of the drive to improve the international response to organised crime. The signing in Palermo in December 2000 of the UN Convention on Transnational Organised Crime was a major milestone, and the UK will be working with other countries in ratifying and bringing the Convention and its associated protocols into effect.

International, multi-agency response – people trafficking

Europol estimates that 500,000 illegal entrants are smuggled annually into the EU, with much of this traffic now passing through the Western Balkans. Many are transported in horrific conditions. Traffickers have been seen to throw women and children into the sea or use them as human shields, rather than run the risk of being caught.

The UK has proposed sending teams of operational experts from EU Member States to work alongside the local border authorities, and the establishment of a multi-national network of immigration liaison officers in the region. These officers will gather intelligence and link with Europol and local enforcement agencies to disrupt the gangs.

This proposal builds on the UK experience of coordinating a multi-agency response to people trafficking, exemplified by Operation Zephaniah, a major international effort in December 2000 led by the UK. A pan-European smuggling ring was dismantled, and a number of arrests made, following the interception in Germany of a consignment of migrants destined for the UK. This response is now coordinated by the National Crime Squad, supported by the Immigration Service and NCIS, through the *Reflex* multi-agency task force, which links intelligence to the operational response.

Modernising the Criminal Justice System

We will deprive criminals of their assets

3.214 Justice demands that we should stop criminals profiting from their crimes. Confiscating assets and preventing money laundering also reduces the incentives for crime, and removes an important source of finance for the continued operation and expansion of criminal enterprises.

3.215 We will ensure that powers to deprive criminals of their assets are used more extensively, so that criminals know that they face a greater likelihood of losing the proceeds of their crimes. A new assets recovery agency will be established to pursue the confiscation of criminal assets both at home and abroad (see box). We will channel more of the resulting receipts into a fund for crime fighting and reduction, and into drugs prevention. We also plan to extend powers to seize drugs-related cash at frontiers to non-drugs cases.

3.217 The Government is improving the effectiveness of this partnership. It will provide £1.8 million of additional funding for the NCIS Economic Crime Unit each year for the next three years. New powers for the FSA in the Financial Services and Markets Act 2000 will improve the consistency with which banks report suspicious transactions. Future steps will include introducing a light touch regulatory regime for bureaux de change and money transmission agents.

Proceeds of Crime Bill

The Proceeds of Crime Bill, to be published shortly in draft, will reform and unify the criminal law on money laundering, introduce new powers for the investigation of suspected criminal proceeds and update and strengthen restraint and confiscation procedures.

The Bill will also establish an assets recovery agency to pursue and coordinate the recovery of criminal proceeds. In addition to using the criminal law, the agency will be empowered to seek the recovery of property derived from crime through civil litigation in the High Court, and to tax suspected criminal assets under powers delegated from the Inland Revenue.

3.216 The UK already has strict regulations against money laundering, designed to limit criminals' access to financial services, and to provide information about their financial transactions to law enforcement. This requires a partnership between the financial services industry, its principal regulator the Financial Services Authority (FSA), professional institutes, NCIS and other law enforcement agencies.

Partnership and effective, joined up delivery

Key measures

Demonstrable improvement in performance against identified national CJS targets could be brought about through:

- **A robust framework for performance management, with a small number of key targets set nationally and delivered locally, and local managers able to access information and expert advice from the centre to improve performance.**

- **Data on key performance indicators available in league tables to help drive up performance.**

- **Common ownership across local criminal justice agencies of joint criminal justice targets, reinforced by greater sharing of budgets, information, training and both human and capital resources.**

Summary

3.218 The CJS cannot meet its aims of delivering justice and reducing crime unless it operates effectively as *a system* and unless it works in fruitful partnership with local communities. Mistakes have been made in the past through piecemeal reform, changing practice in one area without anticipating the impact elsewhere in the system. It is only by treating the system holistically that we can ensure it becomes more effective at reducing crime.

3.219 The Government wants to see a CJS operating effectively in its entirety, providing an effective, intelligent response to modern crime and criminality. Action needs to be taken in three key areas:

- *Setting a clear performance management framework*: with a small number of simple national targets; clear accountability and effective incentives and support for local managers in driving up performance.

- *Joining up criminal justice agencies* locally and nationally and ensuring that they are linked to local crime reduction partnerships.

- *Building a highly skilled, highly motivated workforce* with a shared culture and commitment to the aims and values of the CJS.

3.220 The end-to-end process of criminal justice is a complex one. At the national level, three different Government departments are responsible for criminal justice agencies. Cooperation is important, but so too is maintaining necessary constitutional independencies. Efforts to join up the system must recognise the interdependence of the constituent agencies, while continuing to respect the constitutional independence of operational policing, prosecution and judicial decisions.

We have already started to join up the system

3.221 More work is needed to make the CJS operate effectively as a system. Relationships between the courts and other participants in the CJS are within Sir Robin Auld's terms of reference and full consideration of his recommendations will be central to this.

3.222 Since the Comprehensive Spending Review,[163] significant progress has already been made. In 1998, for the first time, the Government set overarching aims for the system as a whole, and published targets for the CJS in a Public Service Agreement (PSA).[164] The second PSA, published in July 2000, is included as Annex C. Joint CJS business and strategic plans are now published regularly.[165]

3.223 To improve the co-ordination of policy making, we have established a Ministerial Group on the CJS.[166] At the local level, the reorganisation of criminal justice agencies (including the Prison Service) on common boundaries, coterminous with police/local authority boundaries, has facilitated more effective local partnership working. The establishment in 2000 of Area Strategy Committees (ASCs) has provided the means to set strategic direction and monitor performance.

3.224 Much has been achieved, but there is much more to do. The transformation of the youth justice system over the last four years proves that practitioners *are* willing and able to change traditional practices to deliver better outcomes for

society, provided central Government provides the right framework. We want to take the lessons of youth justice reform to transform the performance of the wider CJS (see box).

Setting a clear performance management framework

3.225 The complexity of the CJS and the interdependency of the agencies within it sometimes makes it difficult to find solutions to practical problems that yield the best result for the system overall. For example, cases are sometimes listed for trial without an allocated courtroom, as 'floaters'. This is done so that the court can handle more trials and avoid courtrooms standing empty when, as sometimes happens, trials collapse at the last minute, perhaps because the defendant has suddenly decided to plead guilty.[168] But this practice has the potential to increase the police time and resources wasted in waiting at court.[169]

3.226 The fact that different agencies work to different agency targets is sometimes a source of frustration to practitioners:

Reform of youth justice system[167]

Since 1997, the system has been modernised and strengthened, with:

- **A single statutory aim – all agencies involved have a legal duty to prevent offending by young people.**

- **Local multi-agency Youth Offending Teams (YOTs), breaking down the barriers between police, probation and health authorities to make more effective interventions in the lives of youngsters at risk of persistent offending.**

- **A clear focus on tackling delays, leading to significant performance improvements.**

---

[163]*Modern public services for Britain: investing in reform: Comprehensive Spending Review: new public spending plans 1999-2002* (1999).

[164]*Public Services for the Future: Modernisation, Reform, Accountability* (1998).

[165]*CJS Strategic Plan 1999-2002 and Business Plan 1999-2000* (1999); *CJS Business Plan 2000-2001* (2000); *CJS Business Plan 2001-2002* (2001).

[166]The CJS Ministerial Steering Group is chaired by the Home Secretary and comprises the Lord Chancellor, the Attorney General and the Chief Secretary to the Treasury.

[167]Sections 8-16, 37-42, 44, 47-48, 67-79, 97-98, Crime and Disorder Act 1998.

[168]Almost one quarter of cases dealt with in the Crown Court last year resulted in a cracked trial either because of a late change of the defendant's plea or because the trial did not proceed for another reason.

[169]Research into court attendance found that an average of 152 minutes was spent by police officers waiting at court. Only 40 per cent of officers who attended court in order to give evidence did so. *Court Attendance by Police Officers* (1994).

Views of practitioners

"We have all got different targets. And we are all funded in different ways to meet those targets. Now what needs to happen is not just a joining up of the system. But to measure us all by the same target."

CPS practitioner, London

3.227 So to raise performance for the system as a whole, the Government has developed shared, system wide objectives and targets.[170] For example, all agencies are committed to action to increase the proportion of crimes ending in an offender being brought to justice (see Annex C). We intend to build on this approach, working in consultation with practitioners. In particular, a task force with a tripartite[171] steering group is working to ensure that as far as possible performance targets and indicators are set in an holistic context and do not clash, making it easier for local managers to judge and deliver priorities.

3.228 Getting the right balance between local and national responsibilities is essential. The centre should set standards and direction; local managers should have the freedom to deliver targets in the best way locally. Intervention from the centre should be in inverse proportion to success. Areas that perform well against shared targets should have the flexibility to set additional local targets reflecting local problems or priorities.

3.229 In what we have done so far to develop a new framework, we have listened to what practitioners have said about the strengths and weaknesses of current arrangements. We should continue this approach.

What changes do practitioners want to see?

At the CJS Business Planning Event on 11 December 2000, attended by practitioners from across the CJS, the key outcomes practitioners asked for were:

- **'bottom up' input to the planning process;**

- **clear, prioritised and communicated nationwide targets;**

- **meaningful and diagnostic performance information;**

- **a planning timetable structured so that national plans can inform local ones; and**

- **good practice – what works and what doesn't – to be collated and promulgated by the centre.**

3.230 The Government expects to pursue clearer strategic direction, perhaps by establishing a strengthened Strategic Planning Board (SPB) (including the heads of each national criminal justice agency and a representative from ACPO) to advise criminal justice Ministers. This Board could make sure the annual planning process took account of practitioners' views and was scheduled to give local managers time to make local plans and deploy resources.

3.231 Under this model, Ministers – on the advice of SPB – might set a maximum of three national priorities each year. Local areas would then account to the SPB for the delivery of these targets. Learning from experience elsewhere in local government and the public services, it would be important to develop effective incentives for improved performance, where appropriate, by for example rewarding success with additional funding or greater management flexibility.

---

[170]*Business Plan 2000-2001* (2000).
[171]ie Home Office, Lord Chancellor's Department and CPS

3.232 The role of Inspectorates in raising CJS performance is crucial: inspection can ensure that weaknesses across the system are spotted early and swift action taken, and can identify opportunities for improvement and facilitate the cross-fertilisation of ideas. Where very poor performance is identified, an inspection can trigger intervention. For example, the Local Government Act 1999 gives the Home Secretary a range of powers where police authorities are failing to deliver Best Value, from requiring amendment to a performance plan through to removing responsibility for a function from an authority. Similarly, the Justices of the Peace Act gives the Lord Chancellor power to intervene where MCCs have not implemented an Inspectorate recommendation, requiring them to do so within a specified period. Should the MCC fail to do so, ultimately the Lord Chancellor can exercise his default powers which may result in one or more members being removed from office.

3.233 To drive up whole system performance, there could be more coordination of inspection programmes by the six inspection bodies and an emphasis on more 'thematic' inspections that look at issues cutting across more than one agency.[172]

3.234 We need strong, clear two-way communication and accountability between the centre and local areas. This might be facilitated by a criminal justice Performance and Innovation Directorate, led by the Director of Criminal Justice Performance, and made up of central government officials and criminal justice practitioners on secondment.

3.235 Under this model, the Directorate's remit would include:

- identifying and spreading best practice;

- commissioning modelling, research and management information;

- liaising with the inspectorates;

- offering expert advice to improve local delivery;

- supporting long term strategic thinking and benchmarking; and

- promoting effective two way communication – one way of doing this would be by setting up a Practitioner's Panel to offer a frontline voice to policy makers at the centre.

Encouraging criminal justice agencies to join up ...

3.236 There are great efforts being made across the country to forge more effective links between local criminal justice agencies. For example, as a result of the Narey[173] and Glidewell[174] reviews, cooperation between the police and the CPS is reducing the time taken to prepare cases for court and improving the quality both of prosecutions and of services to victims and witnesses. Sometimes cooperation can be assisted through co-location.

3.237 But more is needed to turn the evident goodwill into real improvements in delivery. The Government sees advantages in strengthening local arrangements, with:

- Firstly, real collective authority for criminal justice agencies together to raise local performance – the 42 Area Strategy Committees (ASCs) have established the principle of inter-agency co-operation and some have proved very effective. But we see

---

[172]The report *Casework Information Needs across the Criminal Justice System* was the first to involve all six inspectorates, ie. HM Inspectorate of Constabulary, HM Probation Inspectorate, HM Inspectorate of Prisons, Magistrates' Courts Inspectorate, Crown Prosecution Inspectorate and HM Social Service Inspectorate.

[173]*Review of Delay in the Criminal Justice System* (1997).

[174]*Review of the Crown Prosecution Service* (1998).

The benefits of co-location of criminal justice staff

A Private Finance Initiative project will provide new courthouses in Bristol and North Somerset, as well as office accommodation for the local Magistrates' Courts Committee. Headquarters for the new Avon and Somerset Probation Service are to be provided at the North Somerset site, as part of the same complex or nearby. The Bristol Coroner will be provided with a courtroom and ancillary accommodation at the new Bristol courthouse.

This will bring a number of benefits – better facilities due to economies of scale (such as shared training and conference facilities); improved communication and exchange of information; opportunities for immediate problem solving when things go wrong; and better day to day understanding by each agency of what the other does.

a need to strengthen and support these partnerships to deliver the step change in performance that we seek.

- Secondly, better links between the CJS structures and local Crime and Disorder Reduction Partnerships, so that CJS efforts to reduce crime are informed by thorough knowledge of local problems and local residents' own crime reduction priorities.

... to raise performance locally ...

3.238 There is some support in the system for reconstituting the 42 ASCs as local chief officers' groups, with pooled authority to deliver real improvements on the ground. Members of each ASC might then, for example, account collectively to the SPB for performance against targets. This collective responsibility would not derogate from individual service lines of accountability. Areas' relative performance could be published in league tables to enable ASCs to benchmark their performance.

3.239 The possibility of putting the new ASCs on a statutory footing will be considered if this would help to reinforce the new performance management arrangements. The experience of the youth justice system and of local Crime and

Disorder Reduction Partnerships has been that statutory powers and duties help clarify roles and aid cooperation.

3.240 With greater strategic direction, each new ASC would draw up and implement its own annual local plan showing how it will deliver national targets. Areas could be invited to pilot different methods of planning and delivery, perhaps building on the current pilots of local public service agreements. An early priority would be setting out plans for improving case management in each area to contribute to meeting the national target for ensuring an additional 100,000 offences end in an offender being brought to justice. Performance against this target will be the subject of a league table in due course.

... this might involve greater use of shared budgets

3.241 Following the 2000 Spending Review, the Chancellor of the Exchequer announced a new CJS joint reserve of £525 million over three years. This money is not initially allocated to any single department, but is to be used by criminal justice Ministers collectively to support new initiatives and address pressures in the system. At the national level, for the next spending review cycle we will extend the CJS reserve principle, to support strategic investment decisions in the modernisation of the CJS.

Maximising resources by pooling budgets

Merseyside ASC identified practical steps to take forward recommendations from its race sub-group, but no individual agency had the resources to take them forward.

The ASC resolved this by jointly funding a dedicated race co-ordinator for 12 months. The police, the CPS, probation, HMP Liverpool, HMP Altcourse, the Magistrates' Courts Committee, the Court Service and Customs & Excise each contributed £5,000.

Valuable work is already underway on developing a support network for minority ethnic staff, building a data pool of recruits, and introducing Positive Action programmes.

3.242 We are also exploring the scope for greater budgetary flexibility at local level, with different agencies pooling funding for specific initiatives to enable ASCs to meet local and national priorities.

Criminal justice agencies could also join up with local crime reduction bodies

3.243 Joining up between CJS agencies is crucial. So too is forging effective links between ASCs and the network of Crime and Disorder Reduction Partnerships, and other local partnerships. They have complementary roles; it is important that they are mutually supportive.

3.244 Achieving this relationship in practice is not straightforward. Any one ASC will have several Crime and Disorder Reduction Partnerships in their area. For example, Manchester ASC covers the same area as 10 Crime and Disorder Reduction Partnerships. However, a number of practical steps can be taken to build up links:

- The 10 Crime Reduction Directors, based in the Government Offices for the Regions, are in a strong position to advise ASCs on local crime issues, and how they can support crime reduction. We are not suggesting that they should be standing members of every ASC. But they should be able to participate in an ASC when they deem that there is a need.

- ASC performance plans should take account of local Crime and Disorder Audits and Strategies.

- Joint training for partnership members on common issues offers a valuable way of promoting mutual understanding.

3.245 Partnership working means that the whole is greater than the sum of the parts. A whole raft of agencies and partnerships have a critical role to play in crime reduction, such as YOTs, Drug Action Teams, and health and education authorities. ASCs need to link effectively with these too. The configuration of successful local partnerships varies from area to area, so it would not be helpful to try to prescribe what these links should be. Instead, the introduction of new Local Strategic Partnerships[175] offers an opportunity to rationalise existing partnerships to make sure there is the best fit locally and the most effective working methods and outcomes are achieved.

---

[175]As described in a Government consultation paper in October 2000.

A highly skilled and motivated workforce

Key measures

To promote a criminal justice system which:

- **Reflects our diverse communities and promotes equality.**

- **Attracts and develops talent – staff with a varied background of operational and policy experience but with the skills to deliver on specific jobs.**

- **Welcomes career paths crossing CJS agency boundaries and enables activities which foster understanding and cross-fertilisation of ideas.**

- **Sees the public as an important stakeholder in the CJS and a part of the process not apart from it.**

3.246 Agencies within the CJS employ over 250,000 people. In addition, there are many tens of thousands of volunteers involved. All have been making great efforts – rewarded with improved performance in recent years. We will consult with – and invest in – this workforce to equip it to deliver the vision set out in this document.

3.247 Our vision is of:

- A criminal justice workforce with high levels of professionalism and skill and high morale.

- A strong public service ethic that promotes equality, welcomes diversity, breaks down the barriers between the different services, and is committed to the core values of the CJS.

- A shared commitment to improving performance to ensure better outcomes for society – fair, efficient justice and fewer crimes.

Promoting race equality in the CJS

The Race Relations (Amendment) Act 2000 places a statutory duty on public bodies, such as the police, prisons, probation and the CPS, to promote race equality. It will apply to employment as well as service delivery.

The Home Secretary published race equality employment targets in July 1999. All police forces, the Prison Service and the Probation Service have set stretching targets for the recruitment, retention, and career progression of minority ethnic staff to be achieved over a ten year period.[176]

The CPS is promoting diversity and addressing discrimination by, for example, training all staff in equality and diversity by July 2002 and increasing open recruitment.

The Court Service (civil and criminal) has a higher proportion of minority ethnic staff than the economically active population as a whole. Targets are now directed at achieving a significant increase in the proportion of minority ethnic staff in higher grades.

3.248 We will be consulting practitioners and the public on the proposed core values for the CJS, as a way of stimulating and strengthening common aims amongst the criminal justice agencies (see draft at Annex D). We will also encourage local agencies to share knowledge, training, human resources and capital assets, as well as targets and performance management regimes. This joint working and better mutual understanding will be accelerated hugely by effective ICT links between all agencies.

3.249 There is already some interchange of personnel and good evidence of joint working and even of joint training between CPS and police or between different prosecuting authorities. But all of this needs to be accelerated and combined into a coherent human resource strategy for the CJS as a whole. The elements of such a strategy might comprise:

- stronger leadership matched by rewards for good performance;

- more joint training between criminal justice agencies and with the voluntary sector;

- secondments and exchanges of staff between services and with the private sector;

- creating jobs that fit business needs, not traditional professional demarcations; and

- co-location of CJS staff where appropriate.

---

[176]*Race Equality: the Home Secretary's Employment Targets: First Annual Report* (2000).

Information and communications technology – exploiting the potential

Key measures

- Online crime reporting during the course of 2001 for non-urgent minor crimes.

- By March 2002, every prison handling remand prisoners will have a video link to a magistrates' court.

- By 2003, all criminal justice professionals (police, probation, CPS, court clerks, prisons) to be able to securely email each other.

- By 2004, police officers on the beat will be able to transmit and receive photographs, Police National Computer data and other case background via the Airwave service.

- By 2004, every court clerk will have a computer giving them access to the case information needed to support their work.

- By 2005, all the main criminal justice organisations (police, probation, CPS, courts, prisons) will be able to exchange case file information electronically.

- By 2005, victims will begin to be able to track the progress of their case online.

Background

3.250 For far too long, the CJS has suffered from inadequate – or non-existent – information and communications technology (ICT). Those ICT systems which did exist serviced only single agencies, and then not always with national coverage. This legacy of under investment and incompatible systems has meant the CJS has provided its services without focusing enough on the needs of citizens, and has missed opportunities to improve performance. It has also led to deep frustration for practitioners.

The case for improving ICT in the CJS

A recent report[177] by HM Inspectorate of Probation found that:

"…most managers were working without adequate information on workload or costs. They were also not using the information that was available sufficiently. Most main grade staff were coping as best they could with either an inadequate case management system or no computerised system even though they might have a computer on their desk."

[177]*Using Information and Technology to Improve Probation Service Performance* (2000).

Modernising the Criminal Justice System

"We can't send the police an email asking why have you done this and not that, and so on. It has all got to be done via a written memo. And that will take two or three days, and then the officer is on leave. So it can take a week or more. If we could send an email, it would only take a couple of hours."

CPS Practitioner, London

3.251 Since October 1999, the CJS has had a route map for joining up the system, the 'Integrating Business and Information Systems' (IBIS) Medium Term Strategic Plan.[178] We have brought the IBIS Board into formal criminal justice strategic planning structures and established the IBIS Ministerial Group,[179] to provide leadership. And a fruitful forum for discussion and exchange of ideas with IBIS private sector suppliers was set up in Autumn 1999.

3.252 Modern ICT is now being rolled out across the CJS, so that *within* agencies staff have the tools they need to do their job better and *between* agencies information can pass rapidly and accurately to deliver justice faster. A significant investment is being made – approaching £1 billion over 10 years – to transform the way the CJS uses information and the technology it employs. Sir Robin Auld is including in his review the role of ICT in facilitating effective criminal justic processes, and the Government will consider his recommendations very carefully before making detailed decisions on the best way to proceed.

3.253 Better access to, and use of, information across the CJS will bring improvements in four key areas:

- Sharing data to help reduce crime and protect communities.

- Using management information to raise performance.

- Improving the management of individual criminal cases for greater speed and efficiency.

- Providing a better service to the public.

---

[178]*IBIS Medium Term Strategic Plan* (1999).
[179]The IBIS Ministerial Group is chaired by a Home Office Minister.
   Currently, the other members are the Solicitor General, Ministers in the Lord Chancellor's Department and another Home Office Minister.

Enabling agencies to share data ...

3.254 It is vital to ensure that the principles laid down in the Data Protection Act and the Human Rights Act are respected in order to safeguard the rights of individuals. But these provisions are there to prevent the unauthorised and unnecessary disclosure of information not to make it more difficult or impossible for agencies to share appropriate information. Data sharing is crucial to more effective, joined up service provision. There is statutory backing for CJS partners to share data and these opportunities to improve performance must be used, while of course complying with data protection principles. The Performance and Innovation Unit in the Cabinet Office is working on a major report on data sharing within and beyond Government.[180] This is expected to make an important contribution to thinking about the way in which information is and should be shared across traditional boundaries.

... to reduce crime ...

3.255 Getting to grips with crime in a community requires the united efforts of many statutory agencies – such as the police, local authorities, schools, health authorities – as well as the full range of community and voluntary groups. But cooperation can only yield effective intervention if the agencies understand the nature of the problems in their area.

3.256 By sharing information, agencies can greatly enhance their understanding of problems and devise better solutions. The Government placed a duty on Crime and Disorder Reduction Partnerships to audit local crime problems and gave powers in the Crime and Disorder Act for local agencies to share information for the purposes of reducing crime.[181] To help agencies use these powers effectively, a guidance note for Crime and Disorder Reduction Partnerships on *Data Exchange and Crime Mapping*[182] was produced in October 2000, and a Toolkit on *Using Intelligence and Information Sharing* will shortly be available on the Home Office's website.

3.257 More generally, practitioners from different criminal justice agencies need to share information about *what works*. Robust ICT systems can facilitate this. For example, the NHS has an online 'Skills and Products Bring and Buy Noticeboard', for practitioners to exchange information, ideas and even request equipment loans.

3.258 The Home Office set up a dedicated crime reduction website for practitioners, offering a discussion forum, an interactive information service, and access to a range of practical resources. Three Crime Reduction Toolkits – on Vehicle Crime, Anti-Social Behaviour and Street Crime Robbery – have been published online. A further 19 will be rolled out during 2001. These give simple, practical guidance on effective ways of tackling local crime problems.

Exchanging data to reduce crime

In Cardiff,[183] the local NHS accident and emergency departments were seeing lots of cases where drunken violence had led to injuries. They shared this information with the police, who successfully made use of it to target premises associated with violent disorder linked to excessive drinking.

---

[180] The Performance and Innovation Unit is currently considering ways to enhance data sharing across Government while safeguarding the privacy of citizens. We expect this will result in a toolbox of procedures which data sharers can use to ensure their processes comply with the Human Rights Act 1998 and the data protection principles laid down in the Data Protection Act 1998.

[181] Sections 6 and 115, Crime and Disorder Act 1998.

[182] *Data Exchange and Crime Mapping: A Guide for Crime and Disorder Partnerships* (2000).

[183] *Unpublished analysis by Professor John Shepherd, Coleg Meddygaeth Prifysgol/University of Wales College of Medicine* (2000).

Modernising the Criminal Justice System

... and to protect communities

3.259 Criminal justice agencies – particularly police and probation services – are increasingly sharing information about known offenders to provide integrated supervision to protect communities. The proposals produced in response to the request for a 'Sarah's Law'[184] is a significant step forward in protecting both victims and local people. The law now requires the police and probation services to act jointly to assess the risks posed by dangerous offenders, and ensures that the public has information about what steps are being taken to protect them.

3.260 Paragraphs 2.61 onward of this document set out ambitious proposals for changes to sentencing to make it more effective in reducing crime. This will require better access to adequate and up to date information about overall sentencing patterns as well as individual outcomes. Within the CJS, shared intranets will make possible extensive and sophisticated knowledge management to ensure that decisions are grounded on accurate information and relevant evidence and precedents.

We must use management information to raise performance

3.261 In any organisation, managers need to know how their business is performing to be able to improve it. The CJS collects a vast amount of data, but it is not focused on cross-system performance. At the moment basic information about CJS performance is sometimes difficult to obtain. And where data exists, it is rarely collected on a common basis. This seriously hampers the ability to identify and spread better ways of working and to understand the impact of current practices on different ethnic minority or other communities.

3.262 The Government has invested £37 million to implement the National Management Information System in all police force areas. The CJS is also considering its future system-wide management information needs in order to focus and streamline the data collected. This includes identifying the best form of 'common currency' – cross-system data based on common counting units using agreed definitions.[185] A common currency would, for example, improve national data on delays.

3.263 Improved electronic links across the system, the introduction of a common case management system and common guidelines on the definitions of input and derived data will significantly improve the availability and reliability of information. This will inform national managers and provide a tool for ASCs to benchmark their local performance.

We must use ICT to join up the Criminal Justice System

3.264 The lack of joined up ICT in the CJS currently wastes time and money and frustrates practitioners and the public. At the moment there is no end to end electronic processing of individual criminal cases. So as a case progresses through the system, the same data may be entered repeatedly by the police, CPS, magistrates' court, Crown Court, Probation Service, YOT, and the Prison Service. As well as duplicating effort, this increases the risk that mistakes will occur.

3.265 Each of the six main criminal justice organisations[186] has a major ICT programme in place, some involving public/private partnership deals. These Systems will have to be joined up to make it possible for individual criminal cases to be managed and tracked through the system, end to end.

---

[184]Criminal Justice and Court Services Act 2000.
[185]*Review of the Crown Prosecution Service* (1998).
[186]Police, Crown Prosecution Service, magistrates' courts, Court Service, National Probation Service and HM Prison Service.

3.266 The Government has commissioned a high level technical review of the best means of joining them up and has put in place funding, amounting to nearly £8 million in 2001-02 alone, to take forward this review's recommendations. For instance, we envisage establishing test labs to pilot information exchange through a central hub or gateway. This will enable us to test and resolve vital questions about system robustness, security and privacy, so the public can be confident that data is used responsibly, without infringing people's rights.

3.267 Experience across the private and public sector demonstrates that implementing joined up ICT solutions across large and complex business areas is extremely difficult. We do not underestimate the challenge in the CJS. But we are working with the Office of Government Commerce to ensure that the lessons from the Government's review, 'Successful IT', are applied in taking forward projects in the criminal justice arena.[187]

The Criminal Justice System will use ICT to deliver a better service to the public …

3.268 ICT has the potential to transform the way public services interact with the public – increasing convenience, improving information and choice, and providing access to services 24 hours a day, seven days a week. The Government is committed to realising this potential as quickly as possible. This is why the Prime Minister has set 2005 as the target date for all Government services to the citizen and to business to be available online.[189]

… providing more and better information …

3.269 One of the four initial 'life episodes' offered by the Government's Citizen Portal, UKOnline,[190] centres on crime and the needs of victims. It pulls together information in four areas – how to reduce the chances of becoming a victim of crime, dealing with a crime, what happens when a case goes to court and coping after being a victim of crime. It also has links to a wide range of useful websites, including police forces, Victim Support and the website for the Criminal Injuries Compensation Board.

Making it work in practice

In Manchester, virtual Plea and Direction Hearings (PDHs) between counsel and judges have been piloted since early Autumn 2000.

An IT-enabled pilot project will transfer plea and direction questionnaires electronically between local defence solicitors, barristers and the Crown Court at Manchester Minshull Street using internet technology. This will speed up justice and enable counsel to see cases through from start to finish.

The use of video links between HMP Manchester and Manchester Crown Court for PDHs in custody cases was piloted between September 1999 and February 2000. It found that video links have the potential to reduce costs, increase security and offer benefits to defendants.[188]

---

[187] *Successful IT: Modernising Government in Action* (2000).
[188] *Evaluation of Video Link Pilot Project at Manchester Crown Court, Court Service and HM Prison Service* (2000).
[189] www.e-envoy.gov.uk
[190] www.ukonline.gov.uk

3.270 CJS Online is a complementary development. This website is being redesigned so that it provides more detailed information about the CJS aimed at three target groups – the general public, CJS users, such as witnesses and jurors, and CJS practitioners. Later this year, it will have links to the websites of individual CJS organisations, and to UKOnline. The intention is to ensure that a member of the public does not have to understand how the CJS is structured in order to access information easily.

... improved services for victims ...

3.271 Interactive technology has the potential rapidly to improve the services victims receive. For example, via UKOnline, during the course of 2001, individuals will be able to report non-urgent minor crimes online.

3.272 In the medium term, the Government's aim is that anyone with an interest in a criminal case should be able to get immediate, up to date information about where it has got to through a range of convenient channels. This will begin to be available from 2005.

... and increasing public understanding

3.273 The Government has also put funding in place to improve the websites of the criminal justice organisations and to establish further demonstrators and pilots to make the CJS more outward facing and provide a better service to citizens. Possibilities include a virtual walk through the CJS, a website for schoolchildren with interactive quizzes, and discussion groups. In addition, the Government will provide web-based support for best practice by Area Strategy Committees. In these ways, ICT will help both the public and professionals increasingly to view the CJS as a criminal justice service.

3.274 The Government is also keen to ensure that we collect and use statistics in the best way to understand crime and make the most effective interventions to combat it (see box).

Review of crime statistics

Current crime statistics need to change. Recorded crime statistics have existed in something like their present form since the middle of the last century but increasingly they are ill suited to the modern needs. The Review of Crime Statistics published in July 2000 contains a wide range of proposals to ensure that future information on crime is useful to the police, local communities, and policy makers.[191]

This will require better use of technology to collect, organise and disseminate statistical data – and a more consistent framework for collecting information on crime. The system envisaged will result in better quality data, of greater relevance, presented accessibly and clearly. These developments – which will be taken forward over the next 5 years and will be integrated with the development of police ICT systems – will help to ensure that our information base grows and can feed into policy development to meet the needs of the public.

---

[191]Review of Crime Statistics: A discussion document (2000).

Annex A
Attrition in the Criminal Justice System

A.1 'Attrition' is the filtering process which occurs between a crime being committed and the person who committed it being sanctioned by the police or the courts (for example through a caution or conviction). Measurement of attrition can start at various points. One common starting point, and the one used here, is after an incident has been recorded by the police as a known crime.

A.2 Figure 1 below compares attrition in 1980 and 1999-00. The total number of recorded crimes in each year is set to 100%. It then shows:

- the percentage of persons cautioned or whose case proceeds to a court hearing (ie excluding cases terminated early);

- the percentage of persons convicted or cautioned; and

- the percentage of persons convicted.

A.3 Figure 1 is a *guide* to how the performance of the system has changed over the last 20 years. The comparison is illustrative only in that:

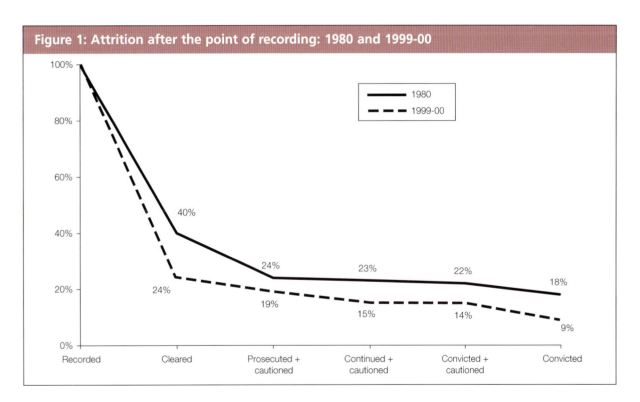

Figure 1: Attrition after the point of recording: 1980 and 1999-00

- The percentage of recorded crimes cleared up by the police in the two years on a like for like basis. (Not all clear-ups will result in a sanction.)

- Then, for indictable offences (including those triable either way – and again as a percentage of all recorded crime), it shows:

- the percentage of persons prosecuted or cautioned;

- The types of offences covered by the two series are not identical and there have been changes in data quality and procedures over the time period shown. (One notable change has been a revision to the counting rules used by the police for recording crime, introduced in April 1998. Another change has been the reclassification of some triable either way offences in 1988, although figures for 1999-00 take account of these changes.)

• The comparison is between *crimes* recorded and cleared up and *persons* dealt with by the CJS for indictable offences. There is not a precise match between the two. Some offenders appearing in court are often dealt with for more than one offence (including offences taken into consideration). This will underestimate the extent to which an offender is attached to a crime. To some extent, this will be counterbalanced by cases involving more than one offender, each of whom has been counted in the number of persons dealt with.

A.4 Over the last 20 years, the number of crimes recorded has increased considerably (by over 70 per cent on a like for like counting basis). This is partly due to increased reporting of crimes for which the British Crime Survey provides evidence. It is also possible that over time the police have recorded as crimes more of the incidents reported by victims. A 'real' increase nonetheless seems evident.

A.5 It is clear that the ability of the CJS to detect and sanction offenders has not kept pace with the marked increase in recorded crime. The number of offenders convicted as a proportion of the number of recorded crimes has halved between 1980 (when it was 18%) and 1999-00 (9%). A significant component of this deterioration in performance is the large fall in the proportion of crimes cleared up.

A.6 Figure 2 shows recorded crime, clear-ups, indictable prosecutions and convictions indexed to their levels in 1958. (Cautions are excluded for simplicity.) Up to the early 1970s, all four measure tracked each other closely. Clear-ups and crimes continued to track each other for a little longer (until 1979), albeit increasing more than prosecutions and convictions. Prosecutions and convictions also continued to track each other until 1980. The fall in convictions was evident from about 1982. The beginning of the fall in convictions in the early 1980s may have been due to the police using their own prosecuting solicitors, who may have been 'tougher' about strength of evidence than the police.

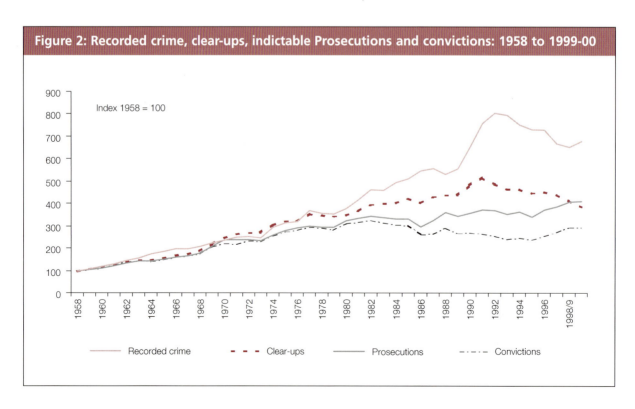

Figure 2: Recorded crime, clear-ups, indictable Prosecutions and convictions: 1958 to 1999-00

Index 1958 = 100

— Recorded crime   ▪ ▪ ▪ Clear-ups   —— Prosecutions   – · – · – Convictions

Annex B

Estimating the active offender population

> This annex describes a model to estimate the number of people in England and Wales who are actively involved in crime. Most will stop offending after a relatively short period of time. However a small number are persistent offenders responsible for a disproportionate amount of crime. The key points from this analysis were presented by the Home Secretary at his speech to the Social Market Foundation on 31 January 2001.

B.1 The Home Office maintains a database called the Offenders Index that holds the criminal histories of everyone convicted of a serious offence in England and Wales since 1963.[192] These histories include the offence for which they were convicted and details of the sentence imposed by the court. Five cohort samples have been extracted from this database, one for each of the years 1953, 1958, 1963, 1968 and 1973. Each cohort contains every offender on the Index born in four weeks of that year.

B.2 By comparing the number of offenders in each cohort with the total number of men and women born in England and Wales in each of the corresponding weeks and years it is possible to estimate the total size of the active offender population. To do this, a model of the conviction/reconviction process has been constructed that divides offenders into four groups:

		Risk of conviction	
		Low	High
Rate of conviction	Low	Group 1	Group 2
	High	Group 3	Group 4

B.3 'Risk of conviction' is an estimate of the probability that an offender will continue to offend and be caught and convicted. For high risk offenders this is 82 per cent, for low risk offenders it is 27 per cent. 'Rate of conviction' is an estimate of the average length of time between convictions. For high rate offenders this is 13 months, for low rate offenders it is 4 years. This means, for example, that out of every 100 high risk/high rate offenders 82 will be re-convicted, 60 per cent of them within a year. The remaining 18 will never be re-convicted. The model assumes these people have stopped offending.

B.4 Similar charts could be drawn for each of the other three groups. For low risk offenders a much larger proportion, 70 per cent, desist after each conviction. For low rate offenders the average time between convictions would increase to four years. In fact, only three groups are included in the model: high risk/high rate, high risk/low rate and low risk/low rate. The fourth group – low risk/high rate – is too small to show up in the data set. This makes sense: offenders with a low risk of being caught and convicted are unlikely to be convicted very frequently.

---

[192] The offences covered by the Index are those on the 'standard list'. This includes all indictable offences (including those triable either way) and certain summary offences. The current list of standard list offences is given in Appendices 4 and 5 of *Criminal Statistics, England and Wales, 1999* (2000).

Estimating the active offender population

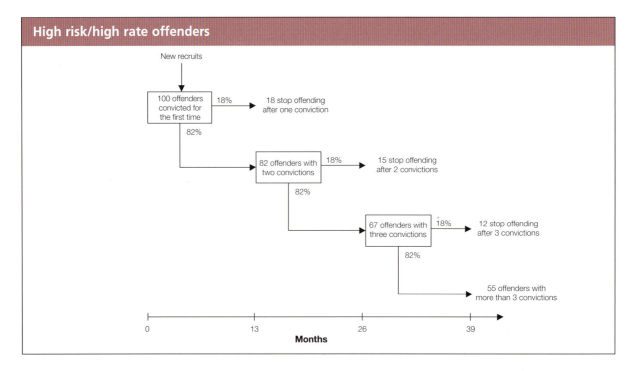

High risk/high rate offenders

New recruits

100 offenders convicted for the first time → 18% → 18 stop offending after one conviction

82%

82 offenders with two convictions → 18% → 15 stop offending after 2 convictions

82%

67 offenders with three convictions → 18% → 12 stop offending after 3 convictions

82%

55 offenders with more than 3 convictions

0   13   26   39

Months

B.5 The model fits the data very well, explaining over 99 per cent of the variation in offending behaviour. According to the model there are about a million active offenders in the general population at any one time. Of these, some 100,000 will accumulate more than three convictions during their criminal careers. This sub-group represents the most persistent offenders who are responsible for a disproportionate amount of crime. Although they represent only 10 per cent of active offenders they accumulate at least 50 per cent of all serious convictions, a finding consistent with previous research. It might also be reasonably assumed that these persistent offenders are also responsible for a disproportionate amount of unsolved crime.

B.6 It should be noted that the active offender population is not static and that as offenders give up offending and leave the population, a steady stream of other offenders replace them. In particular the 100,000 persistent offenders this year are not all the same as the 100,000 next year or indeed last year. The modelling work suggests that approximately 20 per cent drop out and are replaced each year.

B.7 A preliminary analysis of current ongoing research in the Home Office suggests that the 100,000 most persistent offenders share a common profile. Half are under 21 and nearly three-quarters started offending between 13 and 15. Nearly two thirds are hard drug users. More than a third were in care as children. Half have no qualifications at all and nearly half have been excluded from school. Three-quarters have no work and little or no legal income.

C.1 Delivering better public services is about more than how much the Government spends; it depends crucially on how effectively the Government uses these resources. As an integral part of the process of allocating resources, the 2000 Spending Review has set the objectives and targets which Government will deliver, consistent with its priorities for increasing opportunity for all, building responsible and secure communities, raising productivity and sustainable growth and securing a modern international role for Britain.

C.2 The 1998 Comprehensive Spending Review made an important step forward in delivering improvements in public services, through the innovation of PSAs. Through the PSAs the Government made clear it was investing in reform, better public services and a step change in the way they were delivered. This process has continued under the 2000 Spending Review and there are now around 160 high level and outcome-focused commitments that reflect the Government's priorities and its strategic agenda for public services for the next three years.

C.3 These PSAs are a clear commitment to the public on what they can expect for their money and each agreement sets out explicitly which minister is accountable for delivery of the targets underpinning that commitment. The publication of PSAs is of course only the beginning. Every department will be working hard to ensure that the targets are delivered. Progress in delivering these targets will be monitored closely by Government and reported in annual departmental reports.

C.4 The 2000 Spending Review was also informed by a number of cross-departmental reviews of issues that might benefit from a joint approach involving two or more Government departments. This annex includes details of three such reviews: for the Criminal Justice System, Action Against Illegal Drugs and Crime Reduction. The first two have full PSAs. The last draws on departmental PSAs for DfEE, DH and Home Office. Finally, the annex includes the Home Office PSA target for race equality.

C.5 The full set of PSAs can be downloaded from the HM Treasury website.[193]

Criminal Justice System

Aim

C.6 To reduce crime and the fear of crime and their social and economic costs; and to dispense justice fairly and efficiently and to promote confidence in the rule of law.

Objectives and Performance Targets

Objective I: to reduce the level of actual crime and disorder.

C.7 Reduce the key recorded crime categories of:

- vehicle crime by 30 per cent by 2004;

- domestic burglary by 25 per cent, with no local authority area having a rate more than three times the national average, by 2005;

- robbery in our principal cities by 14 per cent by 2005.

Objective II: to reduce the adverse impact of crime and disorder on people's lives.

C.8 Ensure by 2004 that the levels of fear of crime in the key categories of violent crime, burglary and car crime, reported in the BCS, are lower than the levels reported in the 2001 BCS.

---

[193]www.hm-treasury.gov.uk/sr2000/psa/index.html

Public Service Agreements (PSAs)

Objective III: to reduce the economic costs of crime.

C.9 Reduce by 2004 the economic cost of crime as measured by an indicator to be developed by March 2001.

Objective IV: to ensure just processes and just and effective outcomes.

C.10 Reduce the rate of reconvictions:

- of all offenders punished by imprisonment or by community supervision by 5 per cent by 2004 compared to the predicted rate; and

- of all young offenders by 5 per cent by 2004 compared to the predicted rate.

Objective V: to deal with cases throughout the criminal justice process with appropriate speed.

C.11 Reduce by 2004 the time from arrest to sentence or other disposal by:

- reducing the time from charge to disposal for all defendants, with a target to be specified by March 2001;

- dealing with 80 per cent of youth court cases within their time targets; and

- halving from 142 to 71 days by 2002 the time taken from arrest to sentence for persistent young offenders and maintaining that level thereafter.

Objective VI: to meet the needs of victims, witnesses and jurors within the system.

C.12 Improve by 5 percentage points the satisfaction level of victims and witnesses with their treatment in the CJS by 2002 and thereafter at least maintain that level of performance.

Objective VII: to respect the rights of defendants and to treat them fairly.

C.13 Improve the standard by which the CJS meets the rights of defendants, by achieving by 2004 100 per cent of targets in a basket of measures as defined in the CJS Business Plan.

Objective VIII: to promote confidence in the CJS.

C.14 Improve the level of public confidence in the CJS by 2004, including that of minority ethnic communities.

C.15 Increase the number and proportion of recorded crimes for which an offender is brought to justice.

Value for money

C.16 The CJS Departments will define and publish a value for money target for the CJS by March 2001.

Who is responsible for delivery?

C.17 The Home Secretary, Lord Chancellor and Attorney General are jointly responsible for the commitments related to the overall performance of the CJS as set out in this PSA. There are separate PSAs for the Home Office, Lord Chancellor's Department and Law Officers' Departments (covering the CPS) which are the component parts of the CJS and for which, respectively the Home Secretary, Lord Chancellor and Attorney General are individually responsible.

Action Against Illegal Drugs

Aim

C.18 To create a healthy and confident society, increasingly free from the harm caused by the misuse of drugs.

Objectives and Performance Targets

Objective I: to help young people resist drug misuse in order to achieve their full potential in society.

C.19 Reduce the proportion of people under the age of 25 reporting the use of Class A drugs by 25 per cent by 2005 (and by 50 per cent by 2008).

Objective II: to protect our communities from drug-related anti-social and criminal behaviour.

C.20 Reduce the levels of repeat offending amongst drug abusing offenders by 25 per cent by 2005 (and by 50 per cent by 2008).

Objective III: to enable people with drug problems to overcome them and live healthy and crime-free lives.

C.21 Increase the participation of problem drug abusers in drug treatment programmes by 55 per cent by 2004 (by 66 per cent by 2005 and by 100 per cent by 2008).

Objective IV: to stifle the availability of drugs on our streets.

C.22 Reduce the availability of Class A drugs by 25 per cent by 2005 (and by 50 per cent by 2008).

Who is responsible for delivery?

C.23 This PSA covers government activity against illegal drugs, co-ordinated by the Minister for the Cabinet Office and led by the Secretary of State for Health, the Secretary of State for Education and Employment, the Home Secretary, and the Paymaster General. On behalf of Ministerial colleagues the Home Secretary, supported by the Secretary of State for Health and the Secretary of State for Education and Employment, takes the lead on target 1. The Home Office's prime contribution is through effective management of the Drug Prevention Advisory Service and support for Drug Action Teams. The Home Secretary also has lead

responsibility for delivery of target 2. The Secretary of State for Health has lead responsibility for delivery of target 3. The Paymaster General has lead responsibility for delivery of target 4, supported by the Home Secretary. Anti-drugs operations in Scotland, Wales and Northern Ireland are the responsibility of these Devolved Administrations.

Crime Reduction

DfEE Target 5:

C.24 On pupil inclusion:

- reduce school truancies by a further 10 per cent from the level achieved by 2002; and

- ensure that all pupils who are permanently excluded obtain an appropriate full-time education.

DH Target 7:

C.25 Improve the life chances of children in care by giving them the care and guidance needed to narrow the gap by 2004 between the proportions of children in care and their peers who are cautioned or convicted.

Home Office Target 1:

C.26 Reduce the key recorded crime categories of: vehicle crime by 30 per cent by 2004; domestic burglary by 25 per cent, with no local authority area having a rate more than three times the national average, by 2005; and robbery in our principal cities by 14 per cent by 2005.

Home Office Target 2:

C.27 Ensure by 2004 that the levels of fear of crime in the key categories of violent crime, burglary and car crime, reported in the BCS, are lower than the levels reported in the 2001 BCS.

Public Service Agreements (PSAs)

Also relevant: Home Office Targets 3 and 4, CJS PSA.

Race Equality

Home Office Target 14:

C.28 Promote race equality, particularly in the provision of public services such as education, health, law and order, housing and local government, and measure progress by the annual publication of 'Race Equality in Public Services', a set of race equality performance indicators across the public sector; and, achieve representative workforces in the Home Office and its police, fire, probation, and prison services.

Annex D

Criminal Justice System core principles (draft subject to consultation)

The twin aims of the CJS[194] are:

- **to reduce crime and the fear of crime and their social and economic costs; and**

- **to dispense justice fairly and efficiently and promote confidence in the rule of law.**

To deliver these aims the Government has set challenging objectives and targets, set out in the CJS Public Service Agreement and CJS business plan. In delivering these and future targets, all parts of the CJS share the following principles, which express their public service ethos:

- Justice is the highest principle for the CJS: justice for victims and witnesses, justice for defendants and justice for society as a whole.

- The CJS will be open, accessible and transparent, informing victims about their case and the public in general about the system's performance.

- The CJS will actively seek the views of local people on how best to reduce crime and secure justice.

- The CJS will uphold the rights of those who come into contact with it and treat them with fairness, dignity and respect.

- The CJS will work continuously to improve the quality and efficiency of its services, learning through innovation and the spread of evidence-based best practice.

- The CJS will strive to eliminate all forms of discrimination in the delivery of its services and in the treatment of its staff in order to command the support of the society it serves.

- CJS institutions will respect each other's independence and cooperate at every stage to achieve the aims of the system.

- The people working in CJS are its prime resource and must be supported, rewarded and valued accordingly.

---

[194]The CJS is defined here as comprising the crime-related work of the following operational agencies and services: Police Service; CPS; Serious Fraud Office; magistrates', Crown and Criminal Appeal Courts; the Prison and the Probation Service; the Criminal Defence Services; the Criminal Injuries Compensation Authority and other victim and witness support services. There are also a number of other prosecuting authorities outside the criminal justice departments, such as HM Customs and Excise, the Department of Trade and Industry and the Inland Revenue. A wide range of other public authorities and agencies, including local councils and health authorities, also have a key role in tackling and preventing crime.

Annex E

A day in the life of the Criminal Justice System

E.1 The work of the CJS never stops. Hundreds of thousands of staff hours are occupied every day, for example in responding to reports of crimes, dealing with offenders or counselling victims. The following brief portrait provides an overview of the nature and extent of the activity that takes place within the CJS on a typical day.[195]

Crime

E.2 Far more crimes are committed than ever come to police notice: either the crime is victimless and passes undetected or the victim chooses not to report it. It is not known how many crimes are committed every day. However, estimates are available from the annually conducted BCS for certain categories of crime.[196] These suggest that around 40,000 of these offences are committed each day, of which 39 per cent are reported.

E.3 A sifting process then occurs. Not all allegations turn out to be substantiated. There may be innocent explanations for apparently suspicious circumstances. Or allegations may be made maliciously. For these and other reasons, the number of offences recorded by the police is lower than that reported. The BCS suggests that for the categories of crime covered by the Survey, which can be directly compared with police categories, around 55 per cent are recorded. Typically, nearly 14,500 notifiable[197] offences will be recorded by the police on any given day. Of these, around 14 per cent will be crimes of violence, 58 per cent burglary and thefts, three per cent drug offences and less than one per cent will be sexual offences.

E.4 In addition to notifiable offences, the police deal with large numbers of other offences, the largest group of which is motoring offences. Typically, just over 12,500 motoring offences will be dealt with each day by one of several possible processes (e.g. issuing a fixed penalty notice or a report for summons).

The police

E.5 Nationally, police strength stands at around 124,600 officers. Officers operate from England and Wales's 2,099 police stations. Over 600 are staffed on a 24 hour basis.

E.6 Every day about 2,235 stop/searches are carried out, mainly by officers on uniformed patrol duty, of persons suspected of carrying drugs or stolen property. Around 290 result in an arrest.

E.7 On average the police will respond to around 25,500 '999' calls each day. Of these 15 per cent require an immediate response, while the remainder are graded as less urgent.

E.8 Of the daily total of 14,500 recorded notifiable offences, around 25 per cent are cleared up. In the main, crime clearance follows the arrest of an offender and the decision to take some form of official action. Every day, nearly 3,500 people are arrested on suspicion of committing notifiable offences. An estimated 1,750 people are also arrested for less serious matters, generally of a public order nature, or in execution of arrest warrants. By no means all arrests result in official action. It is estimated that no further action is taken against nearly 950 of those arrested each day. Around 2,400 are charged or summonsed and 735 cautioned. (The remainder are dealt with in a variety of other ways.)

---

[195]Many of the figures quoted here are derived from annual statistics. In producing figures on a per diem basis, the following convention has been adopted. If a particular activity occurs every day of the year, the annual statistics have been divided by 365 (366 where figures are for 2000) to provide a daily figure. If an activity only occurs during the working week, annual statistics have been divided by 250 (roughly equal to the number of working days per year, taking account of public holidays).

[196]Robbery, theft from the person, household theft, bicycle theft, vehicle-related thefts, vandalism, common assault, wounding and burglary.

[197]These are recorded offences of which the police are required to notify the Home Office.

E.9 In many less serious cases – particularly motoring offences – proceedings do not follow arrest but from the decision to institute proceedings by way of a written summons. About 4,450 persons are proceeded against by way of summons in the magistrates' courts each working day.[198]

The Crown Prosecution Service

(1) CPS staff

E.10 Once the police have begun proceedings, the case is passed to the CPS. Lawyers review the file and decide whether to proceed with, amend or drop the charges. For the most part, the initial review is now carried out on police premises soon after charge in order that the defendant may make his or her first court appearance within days of charge. Around 1,400 CPS lawyers operating from 96 offices in the 42 criminal justice areas are engaged each day in the work of reviewing files, preparing cases for prosecution and presenting cases in the magistrates' courts. Crown Prosecutors are assisted by around 3,000 administrative staff,[199] including Designated Case Workers who, under the supervision of a CPS lawyer, are able to review and present straightforward guilty plea cases. Although certain CPS lawyers have some rights of audience in the Crown Court, the bulk of higher court work is undertaken by barristers instructed by CPS staff. Each day, around 500 barristers are in the Crown Court up and down the country presenting the prosecution case.

(2) Caseload

(i) Magistrates' courts (including the Youth Court)

E.11 Every working day, the CPS finalises nearly 5,500 cases in the magistrates' courts. Of these, all charges are dropped in around 670 cases, either before first appearance or at a later stage. A further 350 are committed to the Crown Court, either because the charges are so serious that they can only be dealt with there (nearly 150 cases daily) or because in triable-either-way cases the magistrates decline jurisdiction (about 140 cases daily) or the defendant elects Crown Court trial (about 60 cases daily). Additionally, around 450 cases are dealt with in other ways – typically by being 'written off' where a defendant has failed to appear and has not reappeared or been re-arrested within a given time-scale. This leaves around 4,000 cases each day, which are dealt with entirely by magistrates' (including youth) courts. Cases are allocated to one of two kinds of hearing: an Early First Hearing, where the case is straightforward and a guilty plea is anticipated, or an Early Administrative Hearing, where the case is not straightforward and/or a not guilty plea is anticipated.

E.12 The great majority of magistrates' courts cases – 3,930 – result in a conviction, the greatest proportion (nearly 90 per cent) following a guilty plea.

(ii) Crown Court

E.13 The CPS finalises some 500 Crown Court cases every day. Of these, 55 are appeals against conviction or sentence and 95 are committals from the magistrates' court for sentence. The bulk – 350 – are cases committed for trial:

---

[198]These include summonses issued by both the police and other agencies.

[199]The total CPS staff complement is 5,800 (around one-third lawyers and two-thirds administrative staff/caseworkers). The figures given here (1,400 lawyers and 3,000 administrative staff) are lower in total because they reflect only those staff engaged each day in 'front-line' work, as well as taking account of sickness absence.

A day in the life of the Criminal Justice System

Magistrates' courts

E.14 The huge majority (95 per cent) of criminal cases are dealt with in England and Wales's 430 or so magistrates' courthouses with their 1,620 courtrooms. The bulk of work dealt with is criminal, but the courts also deal with certain civil and family work, licensing and fine enforcement for the Crown Court.

E.15 The courts deal with far more defendants each day than the total given above for cases prosecuted by the CPS because some prosecutions are dealt with by other agencies. Also, each defendant appears an average of 2.2 times. On average, therefore, about 16,600 defendants appear in the magistrates' courts each day.[200] (Of these, around 1,200 are defendants aged under 18.)

E.16 Court business is conducted either by benches of lay magistrates (currently there are around 31,000), who generally sit in benches of three and are advised by legal advisers employed by the courts, or by professional District Judges (of whom there are 106 full-time and 169 part-time). Where defendants are aged under 18, their cases are generally dealt with by the Youth Court. Technically, the Youth Court forms part of the magistrates' court service and courts are not usually physically separate from the magistrates' court. However, only a proportion of lay magistrates are authorised to hear youth cases.

E.17 The average lay magistrate sits for an estimated 40 half days a year.[201] Some hearings, which deal with administrative rather than judicial matters, are presided over by legal advisers sitting alone or single justices. The main types of hearing to deal with criminal business are Early First Hearings and Early Administrative Hearings (see above), case management sessions (Pre-Trial Reviews), trials and sentencing hearings. Issues of bail or custody are dealt with at remand hearings. On average, around 240 trials begin in magistrates' courts each working day.

E.18 Of the 7,500 or so defendants making their first appearance each day in the magistrates' court, around 4,175 have been summoned to appear, 2,840 arrested and bailed, and 525 arrested and held in custody.

E.19 Each day, 46 per cent of magistrates' court hearings result in an adjournment. The average case is adjourned 1.2 times. Where an adjournment occurs and the defendant is remanded to appear at a future date, 85 per cent of defendants are remanded on bail and 15 per cent in custody.

E.20 Nearly 600 witnesses attend magistrates' courts each day to give evidence. Of these, around 340 are actually required to do so. Each one waits on average just over 1 hour before giving evidence.

E.21 Over 5,300 defendants are sentenced each working day in the magistrates' courts. Of this total:

- 3,960 are fined;

- 524 receive community penalties; and

- 232 receive an immediate custodial sentence.

E.22 The remainder are dealt with in a number of other ways, but mainly through conditional discharges.

---

[200]This figure excludes those defendants who fail to appear but includes those who are dealt with in their absence, typically in relation to motoring matters. Around 470 are so dealt with each day in the magistrates' courts (the most recent annual figure is 117,000).

[201]Local Advisory Committees are given flexibility to fix the average sitting figure in the light of local circumstances. The figure has to be set within a range of 35 to 45 half days per year, although some magistrates sit for far more than the upper figure while others do not manage the absolute minimum of 26 half days.

Crown Court

E.23 The volume of activity in the Crown Court is much less than in the magistrates' courts. England and Wales' 78 Crown Court centres[202] deal with just 5 per cent of all criminal cases. However, these are typically more serious and complex cases. On an average day, roughly 365 courtrooms are sitting up and down the country. Court buildings are generally open between 9 a.m. and 5 p.m.

E.24 Business is principally conducted at several types of hearing. Currently, the first hearing for most defendants is the Plea and Directions Hearing (PDH).[203] Between this hearing and trial, there may be further PDHs or the case may be listed for 'mention' where particular applications have to be dealt with or progress reviewed. There is then the trial itself. There may be a separate sentencing hearing where the defendant is convicted and sentence cannot be passed immediately. Along the way there may be further hearings to deal with bail applications and breaches of bail. About three quarters of hearings are dealt with by the 466 Circuit Judges who sit in criminal cases.

E.25 On average, around 350 defendants committed for trial make their first appearance in the Crown Court each working day. Of these, about 250 are committed on bail and 100 in custody. The eventual outcomes of their cases are as follows:

- 220 plead guilty;

- 45 are found guilty by a jury;

- 28 are acquitted by a jury;

- 7 are acquitted at the judge's direction at the end of the prosecution's case; and

- 50 have their cases dropped before trial, written off or agree to a bind over.[204]

E.26 Approximately 4,400 jurors are called each day; of these, about 3,350 are required to sit.

E.27 As in the magistrates' courts, where trials take place – and sometimes when they crack – witnesses will be called to appear for both prosecution and defence. On average, around 465 witnesses attend the Crown Court each day to give evidence in criminal trials; of this number, around 225 are actually required to give evidence. Just over half wait for 2 hours or more to give evidence.

E.28 Around 309 defendants are sentenced each working day in the Crown Court (either following conviction there or committal for sentence from magistrates' courts). Of this total:

- 61 per cent receive an immediate custodial sentence;

- 27 per cent receive community sentences; and

- 4 per cent are fined.

The remainder receive discharges or other disposals.

Youth Offending Teams

E.29 A recent addition to the machinery of justice in England and Wales are Youth Offending Teams (YOTs). Membership usually consists of probation officers, social workers, police officers, a health authority representative and someone nominated by the chief education officer for the area. There are now 154 YOTs, covering all of England and

---

[202]Some Crown Court centres have more than one site; in total, there are 92 separate Crown Court locations.

[203]From January 15, new procedures came into force nationally, under which defendants are sent straight to the Crown Court in indictable only cases without committal proceedings in the magistrates' court. There will be a preliminary hearing in the Crown Court in such cases before any PDH. Cases begun before January 15 follow the pre-existing procedure and for these the PDH is still the first Crown Court hearing.

[204]Cases may be written off where a defendant has gone missing. However they may proceed if the defendant is subsequently traced. A bind over involves an admission of guilt and represents a sanction against the offender.

Wales. YOT members are engaged in a variety of work with young offenders, such as:

- assessing and managing the risk of re-offending;

- providing bail information and support services;

- preparing pre-sentence and other court reports;

- supervising community sentences and reparation orders;

- dealing with the rehabilitation of juveniles subject to police warnings;

- dealing with the parents of juvenile offenders under parenting orders; and

- helping excluded children get back into school.

E.30 Comprehensive and reliable national statistics for all 154 YOTs are not yet available but for the 136 which are able to provide information, the scale of activity is of the following order:[205]

- 840 offences each day resulting in some form of substantive outcome (e.g. sentence, final warning or reprimand);

- nearly 300 police reprimands and final warnings;

- nearly 300 young offenders sentenced; and

- 42 of the following kinds of orders imposed each day: parenting orders; reparation orders; compensation orders, bind-overs and fines imposed on parents; and anti-social behaviour orders.

Victim Support and the Witness Service

E.31 The organisation Victim Support exists to provide comfort and assistance to victims of crime. It is staffed by a mix of paid employees and volunteers. The police pass the details of victims of burglary, assault, robbery, theft (except theft from and of cars), arson, harassment or damage to a home automatically to Victim Support. For certain other categories – sexual offences, domestic violence and homicide – referral is made with the victim's consent. Victim Support staff may then contact the victim, either by 'phone, in writing or in person. It is also open to any victim/witness to contact Victim Support and ask for help. To this end, a new service – the Victim Supportline – has been set up and any victim/witness may telephone the number for assistance.

E.32 On a typical day, the police will refer 3,000 victims to Victim Support. Victim Support attempts to contact all victims referred and is successful in 97 per cent of cases. However, not all who are contacted take up the offer of help. Victims are helped in different ways: every day 441 victims receive a visit from a Victim Support volunteer; 67 receive an office appointment and 400 talk to a volunteer or member of staff on the 'phone. Those who are not contacted in person will receive a letter providing information and offering further support. In addition, around 36 victims telephone the Victim Supportline each day for support and information.

E.33 Witnesses to crime – many of whom will be victims – who are required to attend court to give evidence are also eligible for assistance both at court and prior to attending. The Witness Service (which comes under the umbrella of Victim Support) now exists at all Crown Court centres and the service is being extended to magistrates' courts. Currently 28 per cent (114 courts) of magistrates' courts have a Witness Service. Although those assisted are

---

[205]All figures are extrapolated from quarterly data collected by the Youth Justice Board; for the purposes of consistency, each activity is assumed to take place during the working week only, although in practice some activities – such as issuing of police reprimands – may also take place at weekends.

primarily witnesses for the prosecution, the services of the Witness Service are also available to defence witnesses. Every working day, approximately 345 witnesses are assisted in the Crown Court throughout England and Wales. Help may take the form of pre-court familiarisation visits or advice and support on the day of trial.

Probation Service

E.34 The Probation Service carries out several key functions in the CJS, including the preparation of reports for the courts to assist them in deciding on the most appropriate sentence, supervising offenders given community sentences and supervising offenders on release from prison. Nationally, there are 7,520 Probation Officers operating from 948 offices.

E.35 Courts may ask Probation Officers to prepare either a Pre-Sentence Report or, where they have a particular sentence in mind, a Specific Sentence Report. The former are usually prepared within 15 working days; the latter will usually be available later on the day that they are requested. On a typical working day, the Probation Service prepares around 900 Pre-Sentence Reports.

E.36 Every day, around 485 convicted offenders begin community sentences supervised by the Probation Service. The average caseload of each Probation Officer is around 37 offenders on supervision.

E.37 Every day, around 171 offenders who have served custodial sentences of a year or more begin a period of supervision in the community upon release from prison. On average, each Probation Officer will be responsible for supervising 16 released prisoners.

E.38 Each day, a total of 218,342 offenders are under some form of criminal supervision by the Probation Service, whether as a result of court orders or pre- or post-release supervision.[206]

Prisons

E.39 There are 136 custodial institutions in England and Wales, housing a mix of convicted prisoners and remand prisoners awaiting trial or sentence upon conviction. The Prison Service estate is further stratified, depending on factors such as the age and sex of the offenders, the length of their sentence and their security category. Out of the total, 41 are Young Offender Institutions. Eight of the latter establishments hold females. Three are solely for juvenile males (aged 15 to 17), while 10 hold both juvenile males and young offenders.

E.40 Around 375 prisoners under sentence enter prison each day.[207] Of these, 347 are male (267 adults and 80 young offenders) and 28 female (23 adults and 5 young offenders). In addition, the prisons receive on a daily basis around 336 remand prisoners who are awaiting trial or, having been convicted, are awaiting sentence. Of these, 309 are male and 27 female.

E.41 In 1999 the average daily population of prisons in England and Wales was around 64,770 (51,690 under sentence, 12,520 on remand and 560 non-criminal). Of sentenced prisoners an average of 43,350 were adults and 8,340 young offenders.

E.42 Mandatory drug testing has been operating in all establishments since April 1996. In 1999-00 14 per cent of random tests proved positive for at least one drug.

[206]This figure is the total as of 31 December 1999, the date for which the most recent figures are available.
[207]Figures for sentenced and remand prisoners are based on numbers received on weekdays, when the bulk of receptions from courts occur.

E.43 Where possible, the Prison Service seeks to engage prisoners in purposeful activity (such as education and training courses, employment, resettlement and rehabilitation activities, sports and religious activities). In 1999-00 the average time spent on purposeful activity was around 23 hours per prisoner each week. Typically, prisoners spend around 10 hours out of their cells each day (slightly more during the week and slightly less at the weekend).

E.44 The Prison Service employs around 44,000 staff. The average number of prisoners per staff is 1.5.

Mentally disordered offenders

E.45 Not all convicted offenders remain within the CJS. Where the offender is suffering from a mental disorder which makes prison an inappropriate disposal, the court has the option of imposing a hospital order, with or without restrictions on discharge from hospital. Some offenders who are initially sentenced to custody may also be transferred from prison to hospital where the nature and extent of their mental disorder only becomes apparent after they have begun a prison sentence or where their disorder develops after sentence. Those receiving restriction orders will sometimes begin their sentences in one of England and Wales's three special hospitals; others will be assigned to psychiatric hospitals with secure units. On a typical day, 4 mentally disordered offenders are admitted from the courts to one or other of the above institutions on hospital orders. Additionally, about one offender a day is transferred after sentence from a Prison Service establishment to hospital.

Legal Aid

E.46 In the higher Criminal Courts, about 1,200 legally aided defendants are assisted each day. In the magistrates' courts, about 1,300 defendants are assisted each day. In addition, just over 2,000 suspects are assisted at police stations and a further about 700 defendants are assisted under the Duty Solicitor Scheme at the magistrates' courts. Advice and assistance under the category 'Crime' using the Green Form Scheme is given to just over 1,000 applicants each day.

Agency	Outline of responsibilities
The police service	Investigation and detection of crime throughout the UK.
The National Criminal Intelligence Service	Provision of strategic and tactical intelligence on serious and organised crime, and support services and knowledge products, to law enforcement agencies in the UK.
The National Crime Squad	To combat national (in England & Wales) and transnational serious and organised crime.
HM Customs & Excise	Detection, investigation & prosecution of indirect taxation fraud and offences against the Customs & Excise Management Act. Lead agency for reducing availability of class A drugs under UK anti-drugs strategy.
The security and intelligence agencies	Provision of strategic and tactical intelligence in support of law enforcement agencies.
Crown Prosecution Service	The largest prosecuting authority in England & Wales, responsible for taking over prosecution of cases instigated by the police and National Crime Squad.
Inland Revenue	Investigation and prosecution of offences against the Revenue.
Serious Fraud Office	Investigation, prosecution (England, Wales & Northern Ireland) and international assistance in relation to serious or complex fraud.
Immigration & Nationality Directorate	Provision of immigration controls for the UK.
Financial Services Authority	Regulation of financial markets including prevention and detection of money laundering.
Benefits Agency	Investigation and prosecution of fraud against the benefits system.
UK Anti-Drugs Co-ordination Unit	Co-ordinates UK anti-drugs strategy including plans to reduce the availability of class A drugs.
Scottish Drug Enforcement Agency	Investigation and detection of serious and organised crime in Scotland.
Crown Office	Crown Office & Procurator Fiscal Service – sole responsibility for investigation and prosecution of all criminal offences in Scotland.

Annex G
'Turning the Corner': Report of the Foresight Crime Prevention Panel

G.1 The Government welcomes the work of the Foresight Crime Prevention Panel and its contribution in identifying likely developments in science and technology and their impact upon society and crime over the next 20 years.

G.2 The five key recommendations of the Foresight Crime Prevention Panel's report and the Government's response are as follows:

- *The need for a dedicated funding stream to support crime reduction through the development of science and technology.* We shall be working with the new Foresight Science and Technology Task Force to identify the potential benefits of this proposal before making a final decision.

- *The need for a national e-crime strategy.* The Government accepts the need for such a strategy and is setting work in hand as a matter of urgency.

- *A review of the impact of new technology on the CJS.* The Government accepts the importance of ensuring that the CJS is equipped to respond to the use of new technology. Much work is already being done. We will announce shortly how we intend to take forward the proposed review.

- *Incorporating crime reduction thinking in mainstream decision making and 'horizon scanning'.* The Government welcomes these proposals for ensuring that both the public and private sectors consider systematically the crime reduction implications of their activities and will be taking this forward with the Foresight Business and Crime Task Force.

- *Development of programmes to address crime at all stages of a product's life cycle.* The Government fully recognises the importance of this recommendation, which accords with other initiatives currently being taken forward. We will work closely with the Foresight Products and Crime Task Force, manufacturers, retailers and others to develop a 'crime proofing' framework.

Annex H
Crime Reduction Directors

H.1 The nine Crime Reduction Directors for the English Regions and one for Wales were appointed between July and October 2000 to champion the 376 Crime and Disorder Reduction Partnerships. Their focus is to improve the effectiveness of these partnerships by providing guidance and training, identifying and spreading good practice. They also act as a conduit so that the concerns and experiences of local partnerships can be reflected in national policy making.

David A'Herne: Wales

H.2 David A'Herne retired from South Wales Police after 31 years' service and was a Chief Superintendent, serving throughout South Wales in command posts in the valleys and in Cardiff. He has specialised in community policing.

Stephen Brookes: East Midlands

H.3 Stephen Brookes provided 24 years' police service in Hampshire, Avon, Somerset and Leicestershire and subsequently was a member of Her Majesty's Inspectorate of Constabulary, leading the thematic inspection, 'Calling Time on Crime.'

Alan Brown: North East

H.4 As Assistant Chief (later Deputy Chief) Constable of Northumbria he carried out the review and restructuring of the force which helped Northumbria Police sustain year on year crime reductions since 1992. He was the Gold Commander during the policing of the Euro '96 Football Competition and was awarded the Queen's Police Medal in 1996.

Greg Dyche: Yorkshire and the Humber

H.5 Greg Dyche worked in the Government Office for Yorkshire and the Humber, initially on education and training work and later on Government support for business and European Union regional aid programmes.

Margaret Geary/Graham Garbutt: West Midlands

H.6 Having worked in the Probation Service, Margaret was seconded to lead the Coventry Safer Cities Unit and was later recruited as co-ordinator within the Government Office for the West Midlands. Graham Garbutt has been appointed to take up this post from 20 March 2001. For ten years Chief Executive of Gloucester City Council, he has been involved in developing regional structures in the South West.

Hugh Marriage: South East

H.7 Formerly a prison psychologist and later an administrator in the Home Office, working on charities and the voluntary sector, Hugh Marriage subsequently joined the Probation Unit. Prior to appointment he was Head of the Criminal Policy Strategy Unit, which played a special rôle in promoting co-operation on criminal policy and in the CJS.

Paul Rowlandson: South West

H.8 Paul Rowlandson completed 34 years' police service with Merseyside Police and worked in the Home Office creating the Policing and Reducing Crime Unit Information Desk. He was responsible for much of the work that led to the production of the new HMIC Inspection Manual and administered the Urban Crime Fund in Merseyside.

Annex H
Crime Reduction Directors

Ellie Roy: London

H.9 Formerly Assistant Chief Probation Officer in Lincolnshire and Bedfordshire and then Chief Probation Officer in Northamptonshire, Ellie Roy represented the Association of Chief Officers of Probation on matters relating to youth custody and joined the Parole Board in 1998.

David Smith: North West

H.10 Formerly Deputy Chief Constable of Lancashire, in 1996 David Smith was the Gold Commander for policing of the Labour Party Conference in Blackpool. From 1990 he was an assessor with 'Police Extended Interviews,' selecting officers with the potential to fill the highest posts in the police service.

Dr Henry Tam: East of England

H.11 Formerly Assistant Chief Executive of St Edmundsbury Borough Council, Dr. Tam was responsible for a range of corporate policies including crime reduction and community development. He served on the East of England Development Agency's Working Group on Social Exclusion and helped to form the Community and Voluntary Forum for the Eastern Region.

Annex I

Glossary of terms/acronyms

ACPO	Association of Chief Police Officers
APA	Association of Police Authorities
ASC	Area Strategy Committee
BCS	British Crime Survey
BCU	Basic Command Unit
CARATS	Counselling, Assessment, Referral, Advice and Throughcare Services
CCP	Chief Crown Prosecutor
CDS	Criminal Defence Service
CICS	Criminal Injuries Compensation Scheme
CIDA	Concerted Inter-Agency Drugs Action Group
CJS	Criminal Justice System
CJU	Criminal Justice Unit
CPS	Crown Prosecution Service
DAO	Drug Abstinence Order
DETR	Department of the Environment, Transport and the Regions
DH	Department of Health
DfEE	Department for Education and Employment
DSS	Department of Social Security
DTTO	Drug Treatment and Testing Order

FSA	Financial Services Authority
HCA	Higher Court Advocate
HMIC	Her Majesty's Inspectorate of Constabulary
IBIS	Integrating Business and Information Systems
ICT	Information and Communications Technology
ISSP	Intensive Supervision and Surveillance Programme
LCD	Lord Chancellor's Department
MCC	Magistrates' Courts Committee
NCIS	National Criminal Intelligence Service
NSPIS	National Strategy for Police Information Systems
NTO	National Training Organisation (for the police)
NW	Neighbourhood Watch
OASys	Offender Assessment System
OfSTED	Office for Standards in Education
PDH	Plea and Direction Hearing
PSA	Public Service Agreement
SPB	Strategic Planning Board
YOT	Youth Offending Team

Annex J
Bibliography

J

Acts of Parliament

Theft Act 1968

Bail Act 1976

Race Relations Act 1976

Mental Health Act 1983

Police and Criminal Evidence Act 1984

Prosecution of Offences Act 1985

Criminal Justice Act 1991
www.hmso.gov.uk/acts/acts1991/
Ukpga_19910053_en_1.htm

Police Act 1996
www.hmso.gov.uk/acts/acts1996/1996016.htm

Crime (Sentences) Act 1997
www.hmso.gov.uk/acts/acts1997/1997043.htm

Sex Offenders Act 1997
www.hmso.gov.uk/acts/acts1997/1997051.htm

Police (Health and Safety) Act 1997
www.hmso.gov.uk/acts/acts1997/1997042.htm

Crime and Disorder Act 1998
www.hmso.gov.uk/acts/acts1998/19980037.htm

Data Protection Act 1998
www.hmso.gov.uk/acts/acts1998/19980029.htm

Human Rights Act 1998
www.hmso.gov.uk/acts/acts1998/19980042.htm

Access to Justice Act 1999
www.hmso.gov.uk/acts/acts1999/19990022.htm

Youth Justice and Criminal Evidence Act 1999
www.hmso.gov.uk/acts/acts1999/19990023.htm

Criminal Justice and Court Services Act 2000
www.hmso.gov.uk/acts/acts2000/20000043.htm

Financial Services and Markets Act 2000
www.hmso.gov.uk/acts/acts2000/20000008.htm

Licensing (Young Persons) Act 2000
www.hmso.gov.uk/acts/acts2000/20000030.htm

Race Relations (Amendment) Act 2000
www.hmso.gov.uk/acts/acts2000/20000034.htm

Regulation of Investigatory Powers Act 2000
www.hmso.gov.uk/acts/acts2000/20000023.htm

Criminal Justice and Police Bill (2001)
www.parliament.the-stationery-office.co.uk/pa/
cm200001/cmbills/031/2001031.htm

Crown Prosecution Service publications

Philips, C. (1981) *Royal Commission on Criminal Procedure*, Cm 8092.

Glidewell, I. (1998) *Review of the Crown Prosecution Service*, Cm 3960.

Crown Prosecution Service (2000) *Annual Report 1999-2000*.

Crown Prosecution Service (2000) *Departmental Report, 1999-00*.
www.cps.gov.uk/cps_a/annualreport9900.pdf

Crown Prosecution Service (2000) *Service Delivery Agreement for the Crown Prosecution Service*.
www.cps.gov.uk/cps_a/sda5.pdf

Home Office publications

Airs, J. and Shaw, A. (1999) *Jury excusal and deferral*, Home Office Research Findings 102.
www.homeoffice.gov.uk/rds/pdfs/r102.pdf

Barclay, G. and Tavares, C. (1999) *Digest 4: Information on the Criminal Justice System in England and Wales*.
www.homeoffice.gov.uk/rds/digest41.html

Bennett, T. (2000) *Drugs and crime: the results of the second developmental stage of the NEW-ADAM programme*, Home Office Research Study 205.
www.homeoffice.gov.uk/rds/pdfs/hors205.pdf

Burrows, J., Clarke, A., Davison, T., Tarling, R. and Webb, S. (2000) *The Nature and Effectiveness of Drugs Throughcare for Released Prisoners*. Home Office Research Findings 109.
www.homeoffice.gov.uk/rds/pdfs/r109.pdf

Burrows, J., Clarke, A., Davison, T., Tarling, R. and Webb, S. (forthcoming) *Research into the nature and effectiveness of drugs throughcare*. Home Office RDS Occasional Paper 68.

Bridgeman, C. and Hobbs, L. (1997) *Preventing Repeat Victimisation: the police officer's guide*, Home Office Police Research Group Ad Hoc Publication 310.

Budd, T. (1999) *Burglary of Domestic Dwellings: Findings from the British Crime Survey*, Home Office Statistical Bulletin 4/99.
www.homeoffice.gov.uk/rds/pdfs/hosb499.pdf

Clarke, R. and Hough, M. (1984) *Crime and police effectiveness*.

Eames, B., Hooke, A., Portas, D. (1994) *Court Attendance by Police Officers*, Home Office Police Research Series Paper 9.
www.homeoffice.gov.uk/rds/prgpdfs/prg9bf.pdf

Edmunds, M., Hough, M., Turnbull, P. and May T. (1999) *Doing Justice to Treatment: referring offenders to drug services*, DPAS Paper 2.
www.homeoffice.gov.uk/dpas/treatrep.pdf

Flood-Page, C., Campbell, S., Harrington, H. and Miller, J. (2000) *Youth Crime: Findings from the 1998/99 Youth Lifestyles Survey*, Home Office Research Study 209.
www.homeoffice.gov.uk/rds/pdfs/hors209.pdf

Graham, J. and Bowling, B. (1995) *Young People and Crime*, Home Office Research Study 145.

HM Inspectorate of Constabulary (1992, 2000) *Police Forces Annual Statistical Returns*.

HM Inspectorate of Constabulary (2000) *Policing London: Winning Consent*.
www.homeoffice.gov.uk/hmic/pollondn.pdf

HM Inspectorate of Constabulary (2001) *Winning the race – embracing diversity*.
www.homeoffice.gov.uk/hmic/wtr3.htm

HM Inspectorate of Probation (2000) *Using information and technology to improve probation service performance*.
www.homeoffice.gov.uk/hmiprob/infothem.pdf

Home Office (1998) *Juries in Serious Fraud Trials*.
www.homeoffice.gov.uk/cpd/pvu/jsft.htm

Home Office (1998) *Speaking Up for Justice, Report of the Interdepartmental Working Group on the treatment of Vulnerable or Intimidated Witnesses in the Criminal Justice System*.
www.homeoffice.gov.uk/cpd/pvu/sufj.pdf

Home Office (2000) *Criminal Statistics, England and Wales, 1998*, Cm 4649.

Home Office (1999) *Compensation for victims of violent crime: possible changes to the Criminal Injuries Compensation Scheme*.
www.homeoffice.gov.uk/cpd/pvu/comp.htm

Bibliography

Home Office (1999) *IBIS Medium Term Strategic Plan*.

Home Office (1999) *Statistics on Women and the Criminal Justice System: a Home Office Publication under section 95 of the Criminal Justice Act 1991*.
www.homeoffice.gov.uk/rds/pdfs/s95women00.pdf

Home Office (2000) *Annual Report 1999/2000*, Cm 4605.

Home Office (2000) *Criminal Statistics, England and Wales, 1999*, Cm 5001.
www.official-documents.co.uk/document/
cm50/5001/5001-00.htm

Home Office (2000) *Complaints against the Police: Framework for a New System*.
www.homeoffice.gov.uk/consult/polcomp.htm

Home Office (2000) *Data Exchange and Crime Mapping: A Guide for Crime and Disorder Partnerships*.

Home Office (2000) *Monitoring the Satisfaction of Witnesses with their Treatment in the Criminal Justice System: emerging findings from a Home Office Survey*, unpublished interim report for the Strategic Planning Group.

Home Office (2000) *Prison Statistics, England and Wales, 1999*, Cm 4805.

Home Office (2000) *Probation Statistics, England and Wales, 1999*.

Home Office (2001) *Race equality in public services: driving up standards and accounting for progress*.
www.homeoffice.gov.uk/reu/reqpbsvs.pdf

Home Office (2000) *Race Equality: the Home Secretary's Employment Targets: First Annual Report*.

Home Office (2000) *Raising Standards and Upholding Integrity: the Prevention of Corruption*, Cm 4759.
www.official-documents.co.uk/document/
cm47/4759/4759-00.htm

Home Office (2000) *Reforming the Mental Health Act* (Cm 5016-I and Cm 5016-II)

Home Office (2000) *Setting the Boundaries: Reforming the law on sex offences*.
www.homeoffice.gov.uk/cpd/sou/set-summ.pdf
www.homeoffice.gov.uk/cpd/sou/vol1main.pdf
www.homeoffice.gov.uk/cpd/sou/volmain2.htm

Home Office (2000) *Statistics on Race and the Criminal Justice System: A Home Office publication under section 95 of the Criminal Justice Act 1991*.
www.homeoffice.gov.uk/rds/pdfs/s95race00.pdf

Home Office (2000) *Tackling alcohol related crime, disorder and nuisance: Action Plan*.
www.homeoffice.gov.uk/pcrg/aap0700.htm

Home Office (2000) *Technical Notes accompanying the Home Office's Public Service Agreement and Service Delivery Agreement*.
www.homeoffice.gov.uk/pfd/sda2000/psanote.pdf

Home Office (2000) *Time for Reform: Proposals for the Modernisation of Our Licensing Laws* (Cm 4696).
www.homeoffice.gov.uk/ccpd/liclaw.htm

Home Office (2001) *Fighting Violent Crime Together: An Action Plan*.

Home Office (forthcoming) *Self-Report Survey of Sentenced Prisoners*.

Home Office (forthcoming) *A Review of the Victim's Charter*.

Johnson, S. and Taylor, R. (2000) *Statistics of Mentally Disordered Offenders in England and Wales 1998*. Home Office Statistical Bulletin 7/00.
www.homeoffice.gov.uk/rds/pdfs/hosb700.pdf

Kershaw, C., Bidd, T., Kinshott, G., Mattinson, J., Mayhew, P. and Myhill, A. (2000) *The 2000 British Crime Survey, England and Wales*, Home Office Statistical Bulletin 18/00.
www.homeoffice.gov.uk/rds/pdfs/hosb1800.pdf

Mirrlees-Black, C. (2001) *Confidence in the Criminal Justice System: Findings from the 2000 British Crime Survey*, Home Office Research Findings 137.
www.homeoffice.gov.uk/rds/pdfs/r137.pdf

Morgan, R. and Russell, N. (2000) *The Judiciary in the Magistrates' Courts.* Home Office RDS Occasional Paper
www.homeoffice.gov.uk/rds/pdfs/occ-judiciary.pdf

Narey, M. (1997) *Review of Delay in the Criminal Justice System.*
www.homeoffice.gov.uk/cpd/pvu/crimrev.htm

Percy, A. (1998) *Ethnicity and Victimisation: Findings from the 1996 BCS*, Home Office Statistical Bulletin 6/98.

Plotnikoff, J. and Woolfson, R. (forthcoming). *A Fair Balance? Evaluation of the Operation of Disclosure Law.* Home Office RDS Occasional Paper.

Povey, D. and colleagues. (2001) *Recorded Crime, England and Wales, 12 months to September 2000*, Home Office Statistical Bulletin 1/01.
www.homeoffice.gov.uk/rds/pdfs/hosb101.pdf

Simmons, J. (2000) *Review of Crime Statistics: A discussion document.*
www.homeoffice.gov.uk/crimprev/crimstco.htm

Simms, L. and Myhill, A. (2001) *Policing and the public: Findings from the 2000 British Crime Survey*, Home Office Research Findings 136.
www.homeoffice.gov.uk/rds/pdfs/r136.pdf

Simon, F. and Corbett, C. (1995) *An evaluation of Prison Work and Training.* Home Office Occasional Paper

Sisson, S. and Nguyen, K. (2001) *Police Service Strength*, Home Office Statistical Bulletin 2/01.
www.homeoffice.gov.uk/rds/pdfs/hosb201.pdf

Tarling, R., Dowds, L., and Budd, T. (2000) *Victim and Witness Intimidation: Findings from the British Crime Survey.* Home Office RDS Occasional Paper.
www.homeoffice.gov.uk/rds/pdfs/occ-victandwit.pdf

Turnbill, P., McSweeney, T., Webster, R., Edmunds, M. and Hough, M. (2000) *Drug Treatment and Testing Orders: Final Evaluation Report*, Home Office Research Study 212.
www.homeoffice.gov.uk/rds/pdfs/hors212.pdf

Walmsley, R., Howard, L. and White, S. (1992) *The National Prison Survey, 1991: Main Findings*, Home Office Research Study 128.

Whitehead, E. (forthcoming). *Key Findings from the Witness Satisfaction Survey 2000.* Home Office Research Findings 133.

Lord Chancellor's Department publications

Peacock, J. (2000) *Time Intervals for Criminal Proceedings in Magistrates' Courts: September 2000.* LCD Information Bulletin 5/2000.

Lowe, W. (2001) *Statistics on Persistent Young Offenders*, LCD Statistical Bulletin 1/01.

Court Service (2001) *Modernising the Civil Courts – A Consultation Paper.*
www.courtservice.gov.uk/notices/mcc_consultation_paper.pdf

Criminal justice system publications

CJS (1999) Strategic Plan 1999-2002 and Business Plan 1999-2000, March 1999.
www.criminal-justice-system.gov.uk/plans.pdf

CJS (2000) *Business Plan 2000-2001.*
www.criminal-justice-system.gov.uk/strategy_targets/busplan.htm

CJS (2000) *Casework Information Needs across the Criminal Justice System.*
www.homeoffice.gov.uk/hmiprob/infoneeds.htm

Bibliography

CJS (2000) *Criminal Justice Business Quarterly Report: Second Quarter (April-June) 2000.* www.criminal-justice-system.gov.uk/pubs reports/cjbqr200.pdf

Audit Commission publications

Audit Commission (1996) *Misspent Youth: Young People and Crime.* www.audit-commission.gov.uk/ac2/NR/Police/misspent.pdf

Audit Commission (2000) *Local Authority Performance Indicators 98-99: Police and Fire Services.* www.audit-commission.gov.uk/ac2/NR/Police/pipolfir.pdf

Cabinet Office publications

Cabinet Office (2000) *Making a difference – reducing police paperwork.* www.cabinet-office.gov.uk/regulation/PublicSector/ Making%20a%20difference.pdf

Cabinet Office (2000) *Successful IT: Modernising Government in Action.* www.e-envoy.gov.uk/egovernment/itprojects/ successful_it.pdf

Performance and Innovation Unit (2000) *Recovering the Proceeds of Crime.* www.cabinet-office.gov.uk/seu/1998/trhome.htm

Social Exclusion Unit (1998) *Truancy and School Exclusion.* www.cabinet-office.gov.uk/seu/1998/trhome.htm

Social Exclusion Unit (1999) *Bridging the Gap: New opportunities for 16-18 year olds not in education, employment or training.* www.cabinet-office.gov.uk/seu/1999/16-18.pdf

Social Exclusion Unit (2000) *Minority Ethnic Issues in Social Exclusion and Neighbourhood Renewal.* www.cabinet-office.gov.uk/seu/2000/Nat_Strat_Cons/ minority-ethnic.pdf

Social Exclusion Unit (2001) *A New Commitment to Neighbourhood Renewal: National Strategy Action Plan.* www.cabinet-office.gov.uk/seu/2001/action-plan.pdf

Law Commission publications

Law Commission (1993) *Offences Against the Person and General Principles*, Report No.218.

Law Commission (1996) *Legislating the Criminal Code: Involuntary Manslaughter*, Report 237. www.lawcom.gov.uk/library/lc237/lc237.pdf

Law Commission (1998) *Legislating the Criminal Code: Corruption*, Report 248. www.lawcom.gov.uk/library/lc248/lc248.pdf

Treasury publications

HM Treasury (1998) *Public Services for the Future: Modernisation, Reform, Accountability*, Cm 4181.

HM Treasury (1999) *Modern public services for Britain: investing in reform: Comprehensive Spending Review: new public spending plans 1999-2002*, Cm 4011.

HM Treasury (2000) *Spending Review 2000. Prudent for a purpose: Building Opportunity and Security for all.* www.hm-treasury.gov.uk/sr2000/report/index.html

Other publications

Association of Chief Police Officers (2000) *Breaking the power of fear and hate*, ACPO Action Guide.

Alcohol Education and Research Council (2000) *Alcohol Insight No. 1.* www.aerc.org.uk/alcohol_insights/Insert02.pdf

Canadian Charter of Rights and Freedoms.

Carlisle, J. (1996) *The housing needs of ex-prisoners.* Research Paper 178. www.jrf.org.uk/knowledge/findings/housing/pdf/H178.pdf

Department for International Development (2000)
Eliminating World Poverty: Making Globalisation Work for the Poor, Cm 5006.
www.globalisation.gov.uk/WhitePaper/FullPaper.pdf

DETR (2000) *Our Countryside: The Future – A Fair Deal for Rural England*.
www.wildlife-countryside.detr.gov.uk/ruralwp/index.htm

DETR (2000) *Our Towns and Cities: The Future*.
www.detr.gov.uk/regeneration/policies/ourtowns/index/htm

DETR (2000) *Housing Statistics Summary Number 7*.
www.housing.detr.gov.uk/research/hss/007/index.htm

DfEE (2000) *Schools: Building on Success*, Cm 5050.
www.dfee.gov.uk/buildingonsuccess/pdf/schools.pdf

DfEE (2001) *The level of highest qualification held by young people and adults: England 1999*, Statistical First Release SFR 09/2000.
www.dfee.gov.uk/statistics/DB/SFR/s0235/index.html

DTI (2000) *Turning the Corner*.
www.foresight.gov.uk/servlet/DocViewer/docnoredirect=2475/turning.pdf

Hedderman, C., and Hearnden, I. (2000) *Improving Enforcement: the 2nd ACOP Audit*. ACOP and South Bank University.

House of Commons Employment Committee (1991). Employment in Prisons and ex-offenders.

Macpherson, W. (1999) The Stephen Lawrence Inquiry, Cm 4262-I.

Genn, H. (1999) *Paths to Justice*, National Centre for Social Research.

Kangaspunta, K., Joutsen, M. and Ollus, N. (1999) *Crime and Criminal Justice Systems in Europe and North America*, 1990-94.

Jowett, S., Banks, G., Brown, A. and Goodall, G. (2000). *Looking for change: the role and impact of begging on the lives of people who beg*. University of Luton.

National Economic Research Associates (2000) *The Economic Cost of Fraud*.
www.nera.com/reports/show_report.cfm?rid=2160

Plotnikoff, J., and Woolfson, R. (2000) *Evaluation of Video Link Pilot Project at Manchester Crown Court, Court Service and HM Prison Service*.

Singleton, N. (1998) *Psychiatric morbidity among prisoners in England and Wales*.

Transparency International (2000) *Corruption Perceptions Index for 2000*.
www.transparency.org/documents/cpi/2000/cpi2000.html

Van Kesteren, J., Mayhew, P. and Nieuwbeerta, P. (2001) *Criminal Victimisation in Seventeen Industrialised Countries: Key Findings for the 2000 International Crime Victims Survey*, The Hague: Ministry of Justice.

Victim Support (2000) *Annual Report 1999*.

Woolf, H (1996) *Access to Justice*.
www.open.gov.uk/lcd/civil/final/contents.htm

Printed in the UK for The Stationery Office Limited
on behalf of the Controller of Her Majesty's Stationery Office
Dd5069818 02/01 77240 Ord TJ003680